George D. Elderkin

Finest of the Wheat Male Chorus

George D. Elderkin

Finest of the Wheat Male Chorus

ISBN/EAN: 9783337337162

Printed in Europe, USA, Canada, Australia, Japan

Cover: Foto ©Thomas Meinert / pixelio.de

More available books at **www.hansebooks.com**

MALE CHORUS

EDITED BY

GEO. D. ELDERKIN

C. C. McCABE   JOHN R. SWENEY

WM. J. KIRKPATRICK

R. R. McCABE & CO., Publishers
EVANSTON, ILLINOIS

PREFACE.

IN obedience to a popular demand for an arrangement for Male Voices of the many choice pieces of music found in FINEST OF THE WHEAT Nos. 1 AND 2, the editors have carefully compiled and now present to our Gospel Choirs and Male Quartettes, FINEST OF THE WHEAT MALE CHORUS. We believe it will be greatly appreciated and will quickly find its mission in the beautiful service of Gospel Song.

THE EDITORS

COPYRIGHT, 1896, BY R. R. McCABE AND GEO. D. ELDERKIN

FINEST OF THE WHEAT MALE CHORUS

No. 1. In that City.

C. J. B.   Chas. J. Butler.

1. O'er death's sea, in yon blest cit-y, There's a home for ev-'ry one:
2. Here we've no a-bid-ing cit-y, Mansions here will soon de-cay;
3. I have loved ones in that cit-y, Those who left me long a-go;
4. Tow'rd that pure and ho-ly cit-y Oft my long-ing eyes I cast;

Purchased with a price most costly, 'Twas the blood of God's dear Son.
But that cit-y God's built firmly, It can nev-er pass a-way.
They with joy are wait-ing for me, Where no fare-well tears e'er flow.
Je-sus whispers sweet-ly to me, Heav'n is yours when earth is past.

CHORUS.

In that cit-y, bright cit-y, Soon with loved ones I shall be;
And with Je-sus live for-ev-er. In that cit-y be-yond death's sea.

Copyright, 1895, by John J. Hood.

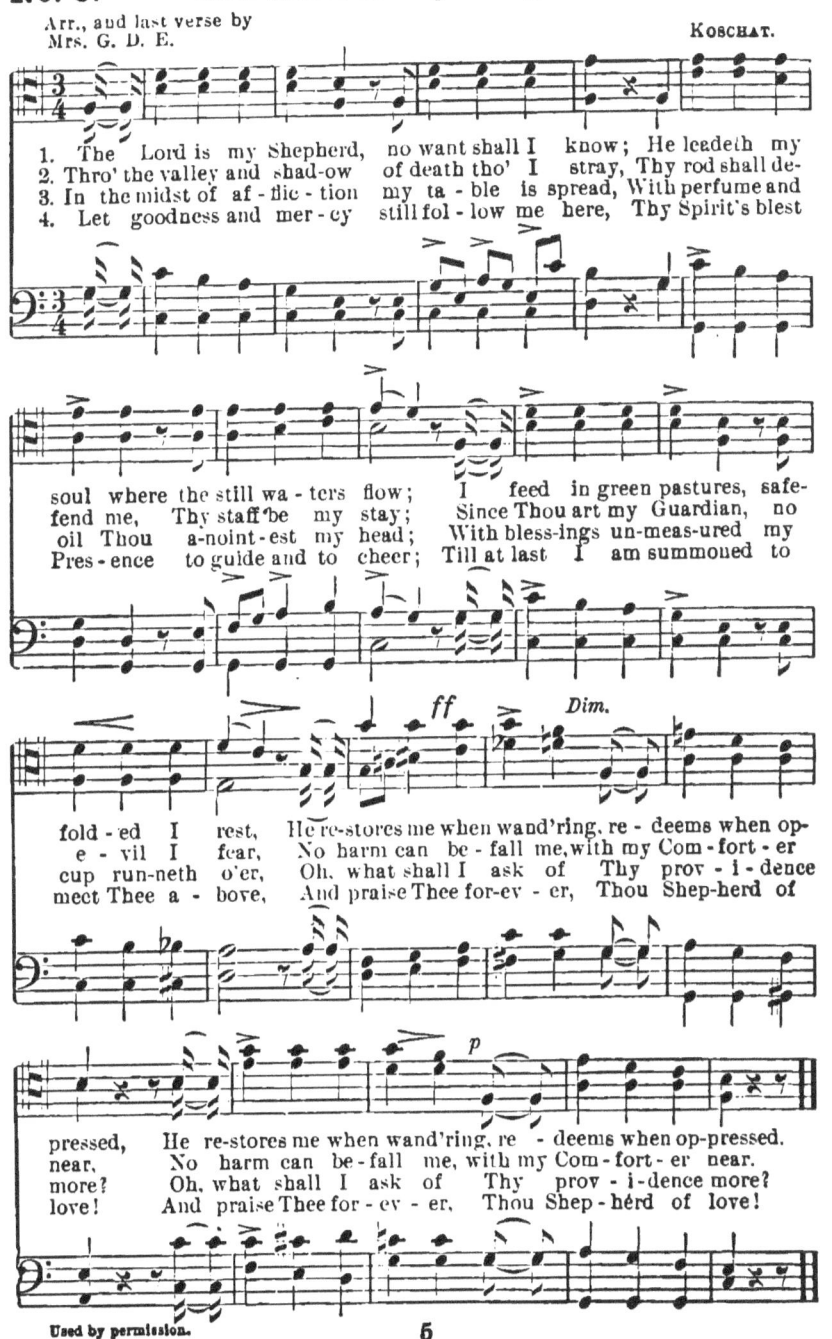

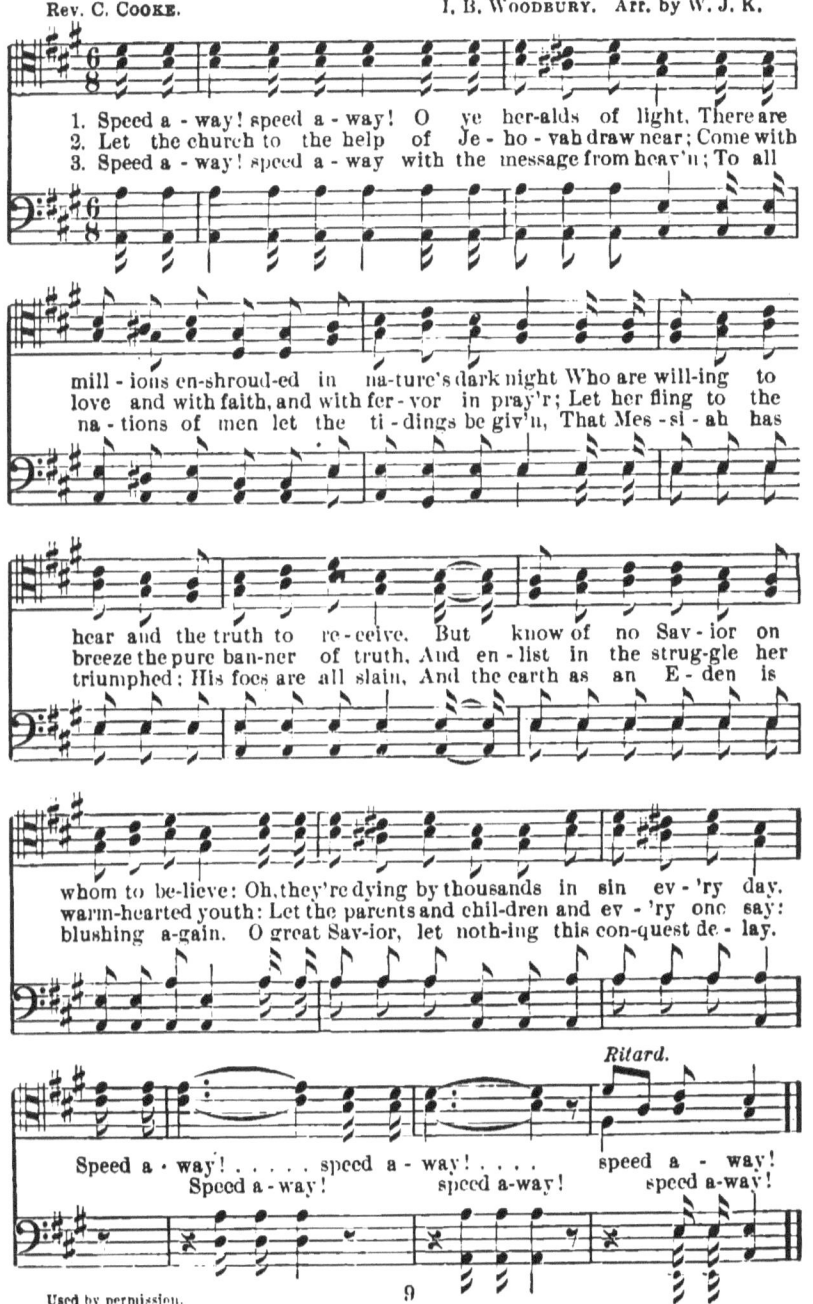

No. 8. Rest, Sweet Rest.

FANNY J. CROSBY. WM. J. KIRKPATRICK.

1. Hark! from the joy-land hear the song, Rest, sweet rest;
2. Still from the joy-land breaks the sound, Rest, sweet rest;
3. Soon in the joy-land we shall know Rest, sweet rest;

ORGAN, or VOICES humming.

Breath'd by a soft harp all day long, Rest, sweet rest.
There where the life-tree fruits a-bound, Rest, sweet rest.
Home where the blue waves mur-mur low, Rest, sweet rest.

Out of the pearl-gates bright and fair, Borne on a sun-beam
Haste to the love-lit skies a-way, Haste where the vine leaves
Rest where the spring-time buds are strewn, Rest where the dear ones

thro' the air, Song for the toil-worn ev-'ry-where, Rest, sweet rest.
ne'er de-cay, Faith on her light wings joins the lay, Rest, sweet rest.
all have flown, Rest where the lone heart finds its own. Rest, sweet rest.

CHORUS. *With great expression.*

Rest, sweet rest, hallowed rest. Song for the toil-worn ev'rywhere, Rest, sweet rest.

Copyright, 1893, by Wm. J. Kirkpatrick

No. 9. **Jesus Leads.**

JOHN R. CLEMENTS.   JNO. R. SWENEY.

1. Like a shep-herd, ten-der, true, Je-sus leads, Je-sus leads,
2. All a-long life's rug-ged road Je-sus leads, Je-sus leads,
3. Thro' the sun-lit ways of life Je-sus leads, Je-sus leads,
                                                  Je-sus leads,   Je-sus leads.

Dai-ly finds us past-ures new Je-sus leads, Je-sus leads;
Till we reach yon blest a-bode, Je-sus leads, Je-sus leads;
Thro' the war-rings and the strife Je-sus leads, Je-sus leads;
                                                  Je-sus leads,   Jesus leads;

If thick mists are o'er the way, Or the flock 'mid dan-ger feeds,
All the way before, He's trod, And He now the flock precedes.
When we reach the Jordan's tide, Where life's boun-d'ry-line re-cedes,
   If thick mists are o'er the way, Or the flock 'mid danger feeds,

Rit.

He will watch them lest they stray, Je-sus leads, Je-sus leads.
Safe in-to the fold of God Je-sus leads, Je-sus leads.
He will spread the waves a-side, Je-sus leads, Je-sus leads.
                                          Jesus leads,

Copyright, 1893, by Jno. R. Sweney.

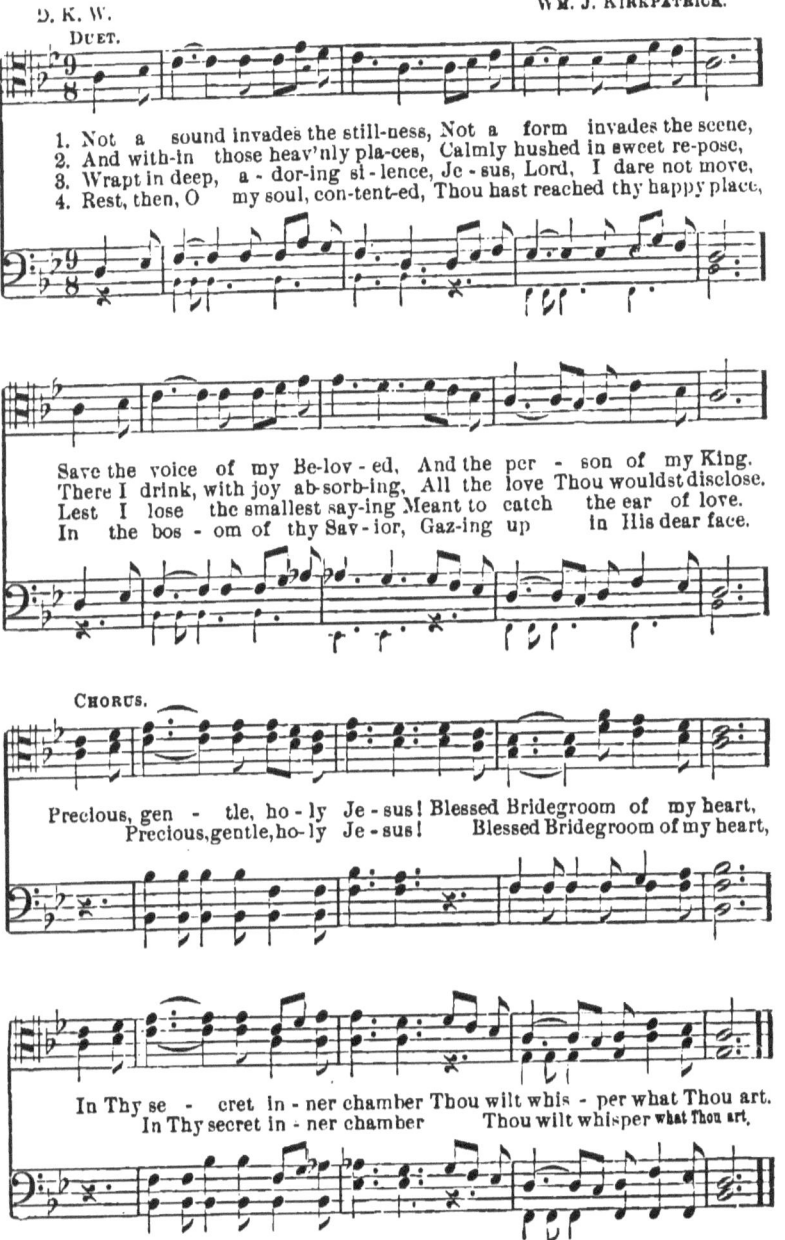

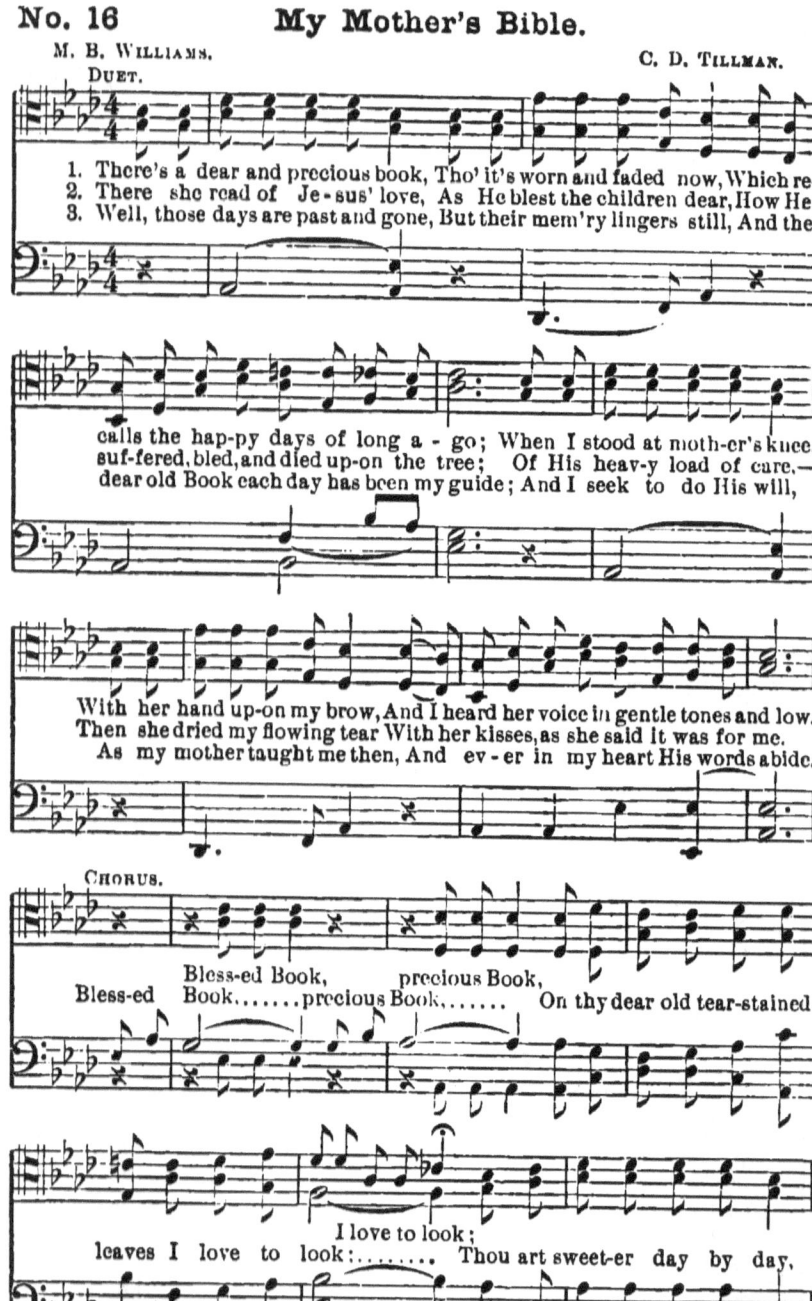

My Mother's Bible—Concluded.

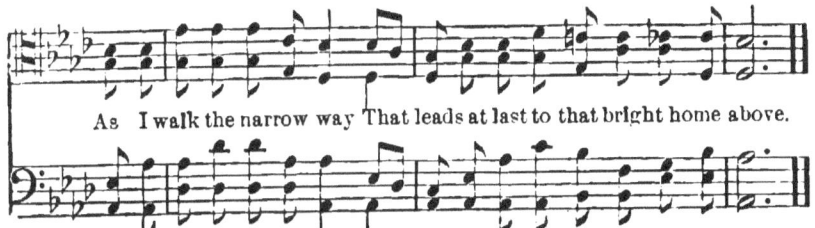

As I walk the narrow way That leads at last to that bright home above.

No. 17. Close thy Heart no More.

FANNY J. CROSBY.   JNO. R. SWENEY.

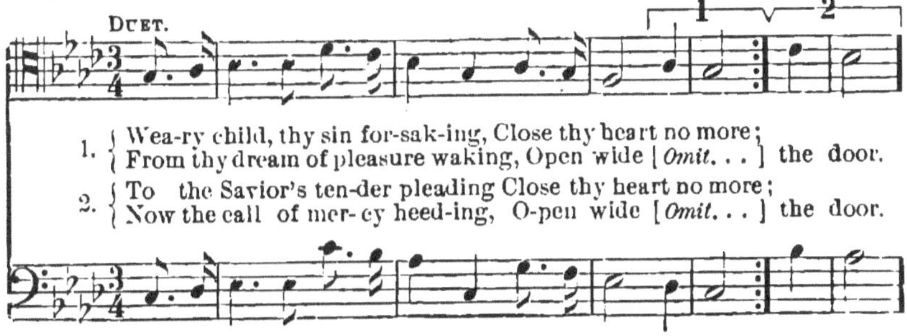

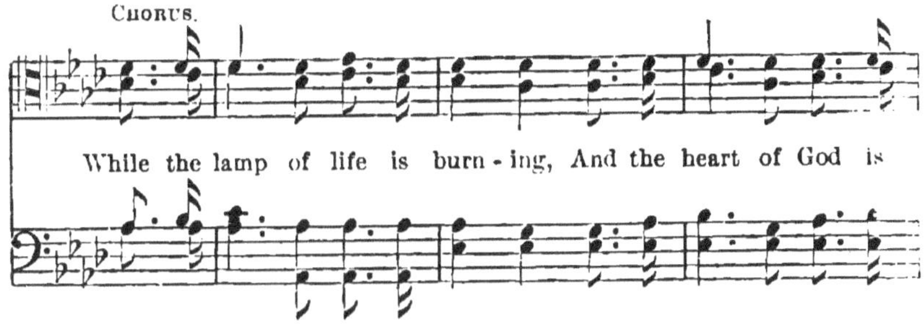

DUET.

1. { Wea-ry child, thy sin for-sak-ing, Close thy heart no more;
   { From thy dream of pleasure waking, Open wide [Omit...] the door.
2. { To the Savior's ten-der pleading Close thy heart no more;
   { Now the call of mer-cy heed-ing, O-pen wide [Omit...] the door.

CHORUS.

While the lamp of life is burn-ing, And the heart of God is yearn-ing, To His lov-ing arms re-turn-ing, Give thy wan-d'ring o'er.

3 To the gospel invitation
  Close thy heart no more;
To receive a full salvation
  Open wide the door.

4 To the joy that fadeth never
  Close thy heart no more;
To the peace abiding ever
  Open wide the door.

Copyright, 1892, by Jno. R. Sweney.

The City Beyond—Concluded.

beau - - ti - ful cit - - - y be - yond, We will sing the new song
beau-ti-ful cit-y, the beautiful cit-y beyond, beyond.

Ad lib.

Of the an - gel-ic throng In the beau-ti-ful cit - y be - yond......
the cit - y be-yond.

No. 19. No, Not Despairingly.

JNO. R. SWENEY.

Andante.

1. No, not de-spair-ing-ly Come I to Thee; No, not distrust-ing-ly
2. Lord, I con-fess to Thee Sad - ly my sin! Now, tell I all to Thee,
3. Faithful and just art Thou, for - giv-ing all, Lov - ing and kind art Thou,

Melody in 1st Bass.

Bend I the knee; Sin hath gone o - ver me, Yet this is
All I have been; Purge Thou my sin a - way, Wash Thou my
When sor-rows call; Lord, let the cleansing blood, Let the dear

still my plea: Je - sus hath died for me, Je - sus hath died.
soul this day, Take Thou my sin a - way; Lord, make me clean.
heal - ing flood, Blood of the Lamb of God, Pass o'er my soul.

Copyright, 1874, by Jno. R. Sweney.

No. 23. Coming To-day.

FANNY J. CROSBY. JNO. R. SWENEY.

1. Out on the des-ert, look-ing, look-ing, Sin-ner, 'tis Je-sus
2. Still He is wait-ing, wait-ing, wait-ing, Oh, what com-pas-sion
3. Lov-ing-ly plead-ing, plead-ing, plead ing. Mer-cy, tho' slight-ed,
4. Spir-its in glo-ry, watch-ing, watch-ing, Long to be-hold thee

look-ing for thee; Ten-der-ly call-ing, call-ing, call-ing,
beams in His eye; Hear Him re-peat-ing gen-tly, gen-tly,
bears with thee yet; Thou canst be hap-py, hap-py, hap-py,
safe in the fold; An-gels are wait-ing. wait-ing, wait-ing,

CHORUS.

Hith-er, thou lost one, oh, come un-to me.
Come to thy Sav-ior, oh, why wilt thou die?
Come, ere thy life-star for-ev-er shall set.
When shall thy sto-ry with rap-ture be told?

Je-sus is look-ing, Je-sus is call-ing, Why dost thou lin-ger, why tar-ry a-way?

Run to Him quickly, say to Him gladly, Lord, I am coming, coming to-day.

Copyright, 1880, by John J. Hood.

It was Spoken for the Master—Concluded.

To the fold of grace may gather Souls of which we lit-tle dream.

No. 25. Keep me Ever.

SALLIE M. SMITH.   JNO. R. SWENEY.

1. In Thy per-fect peace di-vine, Keep, oh, keep me ev - er;
2. At my post of du - ty still Keep, oh, keep me ev - er;
3. 'Neath Thy all-pro-tect-ing wings, Keep, oh, keep me ev - er;
4. Till my last, ex - pir-ing breath, Keep, oh, keep me ev - er;

Where my faith will brightest shine, Keep, oh, keep me ev - er.
Learn-ing there Thy right-eous will, Keep, oh, keep me ev - er.
By the soul-re-fresh-ing springs, Keep, oh, keep me ev - er.
Thine in life, and Thine in death, Keep, oh, keep me ev - er.

CHORUS.

Let Thy heart my dwell-ing be, Let Thy word a - bide in me;

In the path that leads to Thee, Keep, oh, keep me ev - er.

Copyright, 1885, by Jno. R. Sweney.

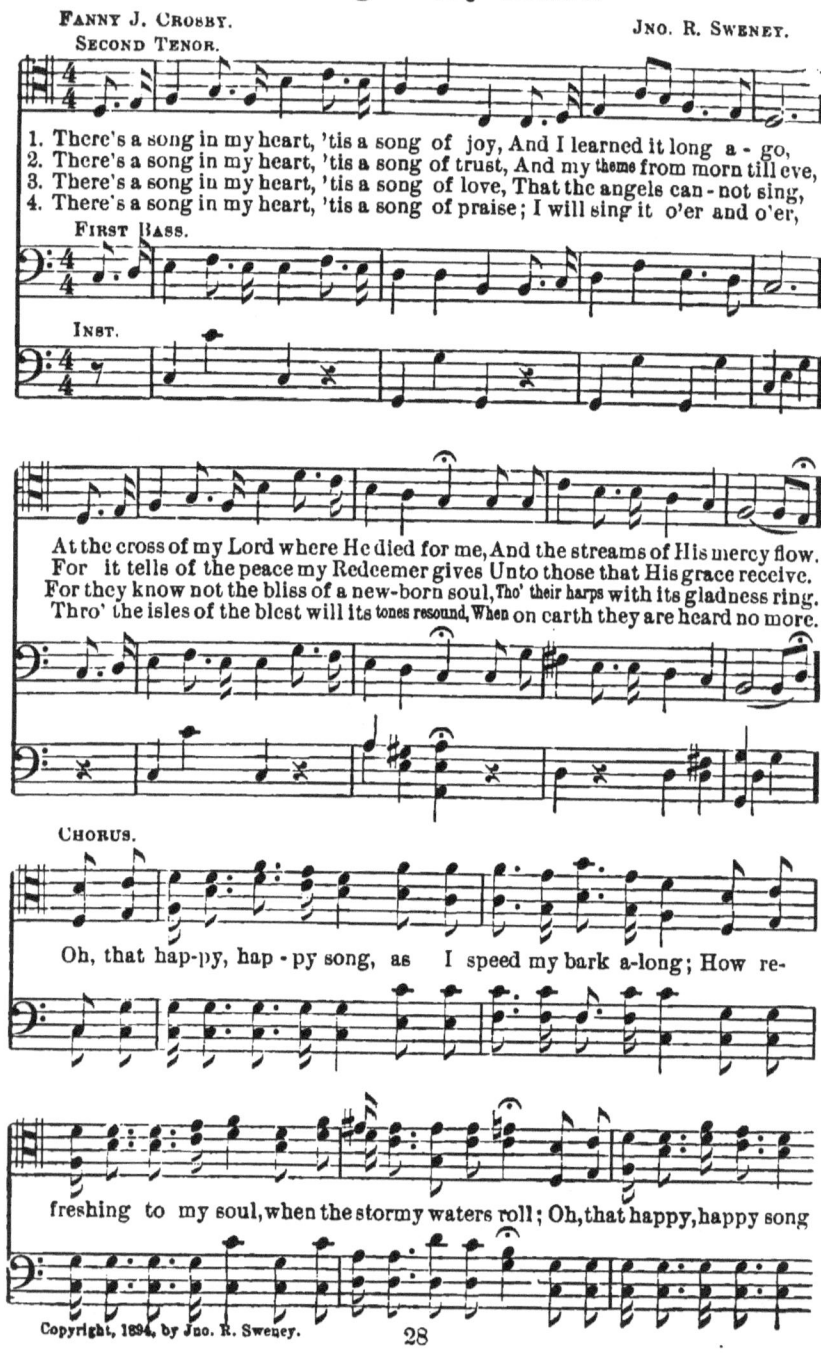

Bless the Lord, My Soul—Concluded.

who .... His face be-hold; ...... Thro' .... His great do-
All His hosts adore Him who His face behold; Thro' His great dominion, while the

min - ion, while .... the a - ges roll,   All His works shall
a - ges roll, Thro' His great dominion, while the a-ges roll,

praise Him, all His works shall praise Him, All His works shall praise Him, Bless the Lord, my soul.

No. 29. Light after Darkness.

DUET. JNO. R. SWENEY.

1. Light aft-er darkness, Gain after loss, Strength after weakness, Crown after cross,
2. Sheaves after sowing, Sun after rain, Sight aft-er mystery, Peace after pain,
3. Near aft-er distant, Gleam after gloom, Love after loneliness, Life after tomb;

Rit.

Sweet aft-er bit-ter, Hope after fears, Home after wandering, Praise after tears.
Joy aft-er sor-row, Calm after blast, Rest aft-er weariness, Sweet rest at last.
Aft-er long ag-o-ny, Rapture of bliss: Right was the pathway Leading to this.

From "Goodly Pearls." Used by per.

No. 30. God Bless My Boy.

Mrs. S. F. A. Higgins.   Geo. C. Stebbins.

1. When shining stars,...... their vig-ils keep,......... And all the world..... is hushed in sleep,........ 'Tis then I breathe.... this pray'r so deep—..... God bless,(oh, bless,)my boy to-night,(to-night.)
2. I know not where...... his head may lie,.......... Perchance beneath,...... the o-pen sky;......... But this I ween,...... God's watchful eye...... Can see.... my boy to-night,(to-night.)
3. As pass the days,...... the months and years,....... With all the change,.... the hopes and fears,........ God make each step...... of du-ty clear,...... And keep... his hon-or bright,(honor bright.)
4. And when at last........ his work is o'er,.......... And earthly toil........ shall be no more,........ May an-gels guide... him to the shore..... Where there... shall be no night,(no night.)

Chorus.

God bless my boy, oh, bless my boy, And keep ... his footsteps right; And keep

Copyright, 1888, by Ira D. Sankey.

God Bless My Boy.—Concluded.

God bless my boy, oh, bless my boy, God save.. my boy to-night.
oh, save

No. 31. Lord, I'm Coming Home.

W. J. K.
Melody in 2d Tenor.
WM. J. KIRKPATRICK.

1. I've wandered far a-way from God, Now I'm coming home;
2. I've wast-ed man-y pre-cious years, Now I'm coming home;
3. I'm tired of sin and stray-ing, Lord, Now I'm coming home;
4. My soul is sick, my heart is sore, Now I'm coming home;

FINE.

The paths of sin too long I've trod, Lord, I'm coming home.
I now re-pent with bit-ter tears, Lord, I'm coming home.
I'll trust Thy love, be-lieve Thy word, Lord, I'm coming home.
My strength re-new, my hope re-store, Lord, I'm coming home.

D. S.—O-pen wide Thine arms of love, Lord, I'm com-ing home.

CHORUS.
D. S.

Com-ing home, com-ing home, Nev-er more to roam;

5 My only hope, my only plea,
Now I'm coming home.
That Jesus died, and died for me,
Lord, I'm coming home.

6 I need His cleansing blood, I know,
Now I'm coming home;
Oh, wash me whiter than the snow,
Lord, I'm coming home.

Copyright, 1892, by Wm. J. Kirkpatrick.

No. 32. Victory through Grace.

SALLIE MARTIN.   JNO. R. SWENEY.

1. Conquering now and still to conquer, Rideth a King in His might,
2. Conquering now and still to conquer, Who is this won-der-ful King?
3. Conquering now and still to conquer, Je-sus, Thou Ru-ler of all,

Leading the host of all the faithful In-to the midst of the fight;
Whence are the ar-mies which He leadeth While of His glo-ry they sing?
Thrones and their sceptres all shall per-ish, Crowns and their splendor shall fall,

See them with courage ad-vanc-ing, Clad in their bril-liant ar-ray,
He is our Lord and Re-deem-er, Sav-ior and Mon-arch di-vine,
Yet shall the ar-mies Thou lead-est, Faithful and true to the last,

Shouting the name of their Lead-er, Hear them ex-ult-ing-ly say;
They are the stars that for-ev-er Bright in His kingdom will shine.
Find in Thy mansions e-ter-nal Rest when their warfare is past.

CHORUS.

Not to the strong is the bat-tle, Not to the swift is the race,

Copyright, 1890, by Jno. R. Sweney.

Victory through Grace—Concluded.

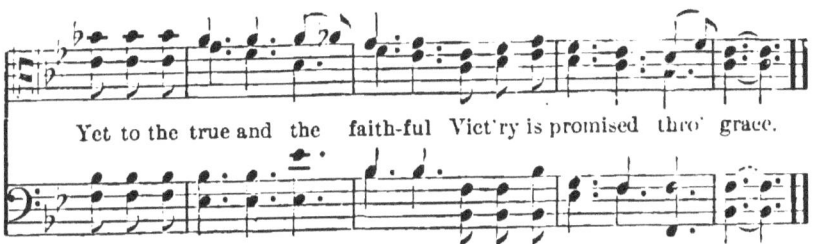

Yet to the true and the faith-ful Vict'ry is promised thro' grace.

No. 33. I Know that My Redeemer Lives.

Rev. H. A. MERRILL, alt.

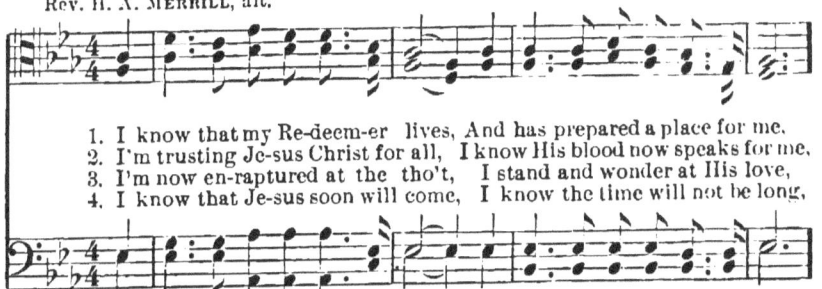

1. I know that my Re-deem-er lives, And has prepared a place for me.
2. I'm trusting Je-sus Christ for all, I know His blood now speaks for me,
3. I'm now en-raptured at the tho't, I stand and wonder at His love,
4. I know that Je-sus soon will come, I know the time will not be long,

D. C.—I on - ly wait the welcome call, To hear the summons: "Child, come home!"

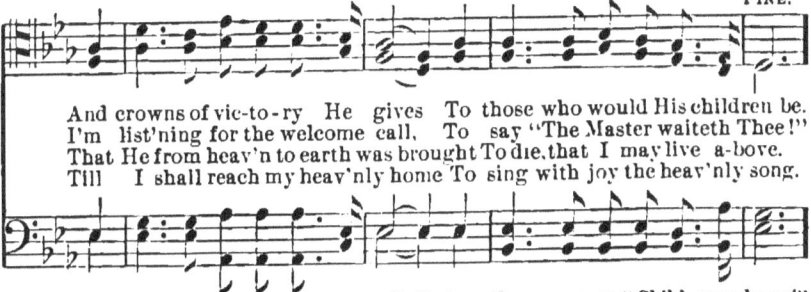

And crowns of vic-to-ry He gives To those who would His children be.
I'm list'ning for the welcome call, To say "The Master waiteth Thee!"
That He from heav'n to earth was brought To die, that I may live a-bove.
Till I shall reach my heav'nly home To sing with joy the heav'nly song.

I on - ly wait the wel-come call, To hear the summons: "Child, come home!"

CHORUS. D. C.

Then ask me not to lin-ger long A-mid the gay and thoughtless throng,

No. 34. I Heard the Voice of Jesus Say.

HORATIUS BONAR.   WM. G. FISCHER.

1. I heard the voice of Je-sus say, "Come un-to me and rest;
Lay down, thou wea-ry one, lay down Thy head up-on my breast."
I came to Je-sus as I was, Wea-ry, and worn, and sad;
I found in Him a rest-ing-place, And He has made me glad.

2. I heard the voice of Je-sus say, "Be-hold, I free-ly give
The liv-ing wa-ter; thirst-y one, Stoop down, and drink, and live."
I came to Je-sus, and I drank Of that life-giv-ing stream;
My thirst was quenched, my soul revived, And now I live in Him.

3. I heard the voice of Je-sus say, "I am this dark world's light;
Look un-to me; thy morn shall rise, And all thy day be bright."
I looked to Je-sus and I found In Him my Star, my Sun;
And in that light of life I'll walk Till all my jour-ney's done.

Copyright, 1896, by Wm. G. Fischer.

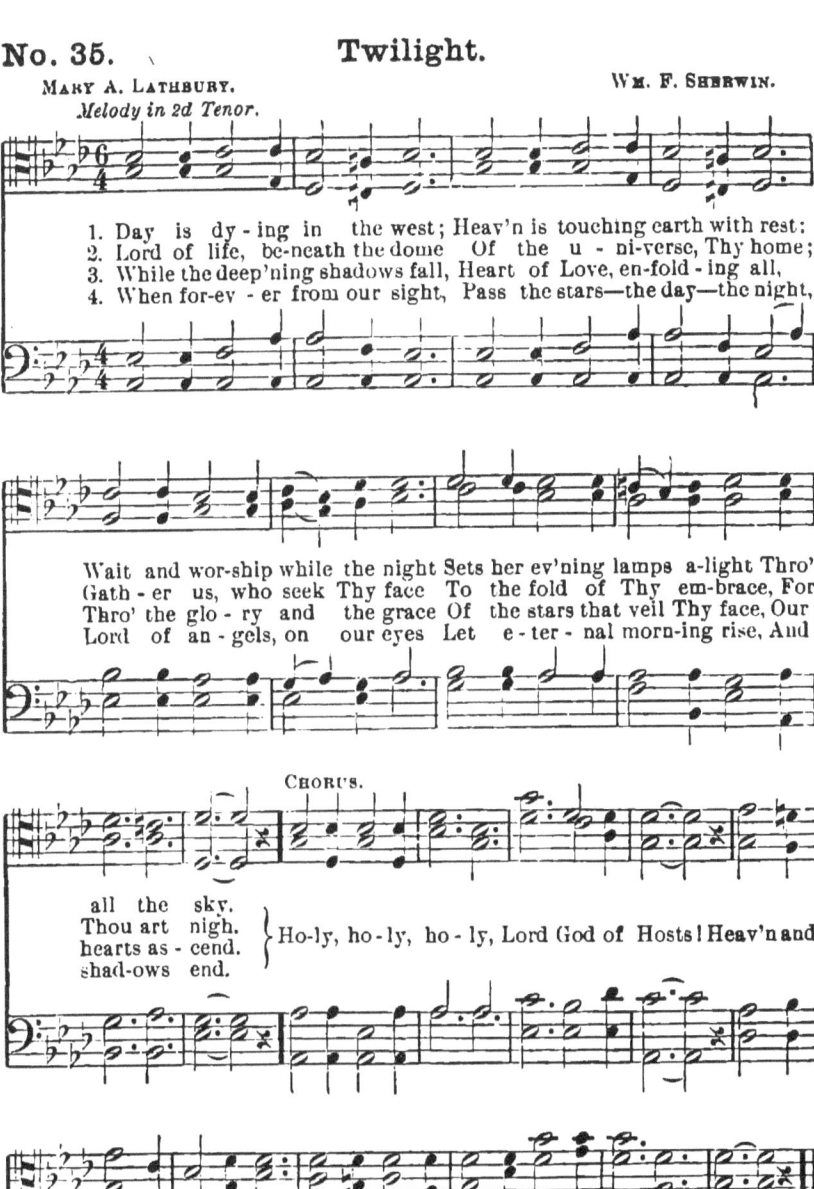

No. 36. Remembered Blessings.

Words and Melody by Geo. L. Brown. Arr. by Wm. J. Kirkpatrick.
Melody in 2d Tenor.

1. I sang, one day a sad sweet song,'Twas at the twi-light hour;
2. So filled was I, I sang no more, My heart o'erflowed with bliss;
3. Thus, oft my Sav-ior comes to me, When all is lone and still;
4. I praise the Lord the fire still burns With Pen-te-cos-tal flame;

A flame of love came gen-tly down— I felt its melt-ing power.
With tear-ful eye and throb-bing breast I knelt in thank-ful-ness.
Each bless-ing makes me long the more To do His ho-ly will.
The al-tar of my soul's a-glow, All glo-ry to His name.

Chorus.

Oh, the bless-ing and the pow-er that the Lord gave me then, I nev-er shall for-get, I nev-er shall for-get; E-ven now 'tis stealing o-ver me a-gain and a-gain, It lin-gers with me yet.

Copyright, 1893, by Wm. J. Kirkpatrick.

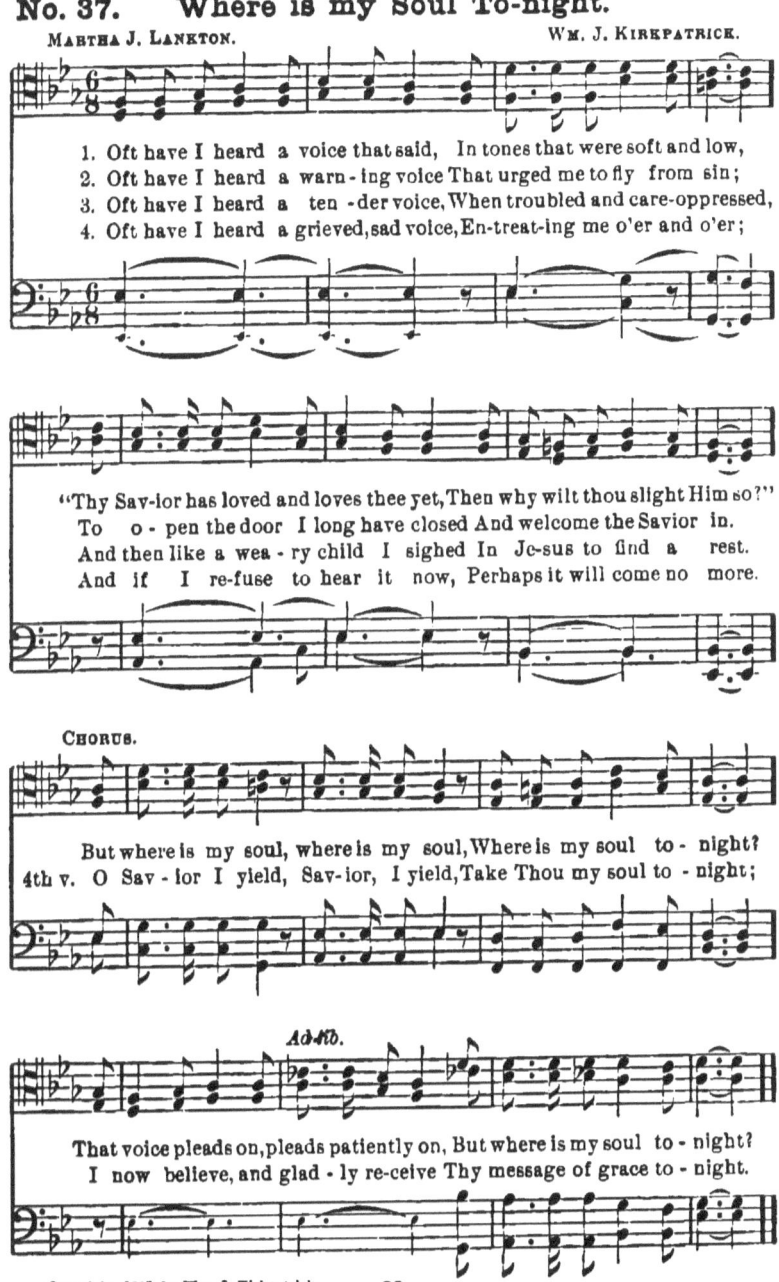

Beautiful Robes—Concluded.

Gar - - ments of light,...... love - - ly and bright,....
Garments of light, garments of light, Lovely and bright, lovely and bright,

Rit.

Walk-ing with Je - sus in white. Beau-ti - ful robes we shall wear.

No. 41.   **The Golden Key.**

JNO. R. SWENEY.

1. Pray'r is the key For the bending knee To open the morn's first hours;
2. Not a soul so sad, Nor a heart so glad, When cometh the shades of night,
3. Take the golden key In your hand and see, As the night tide drifts a-way.

See the incense rise To the starry skies, Like per-fume from the flow'rs.
But the daybreak song Will the joy prolong, And some darkness turn to light.
How its blessed hold Is a crown of gold, Thro' the wea-ry hours of day.

4 When the shadows fall,
  And the vesper call
Is sobbing its low refrain,
  'Tis a garland sweet
  To the toil dent feet,
And an antidote for pain.

5 Soon the year's dark door
  Shall be shut no more:
Life's tears shall be wiped away,
  As the pearl gates swing,
  And the gold harps ring,
And the sun unsheathe for aye.

Copyright, 1875, by John J. Hood.

No. 44. He's Mighty to Save.

E. E. HEWITT.   W. J. KIRKPATRICK.

DUET. Ad lib.

1. Je - sus is wait-ing His grace to be-stow; Sin, "red like crimson," He
2. Standing a - lone in the strife we shall fail; Close to our Lead-er His
3. Take Him the burden that weighs on your heart, Take Him the trouble, He'll
4. Up from the val - ley the darkness is gone, When Je-sus brings there the

makes white as snow; Lov-ing us free-ly, His life-blood He gave;
might will pre-vail; Or if a bless-ing for oth-ers we crave,
com - fort im - part: Held by His hand, we can walk on the wave;
beau - ty of dawn; Vic-t'ry, glad vic-t'ry we sing o'er the grave!

CHORUS.

Bless - ed Re-deem-er! He's might-y to save.
Pray on, be - liev-ing,—He's might-y to save.
Look up to Je - sus, He's might-y to save.
Glo - ry to Je - sus, He's might-y to save.

Mighty to save, might-y to save. Je - sus is might-y to save; is might-y to save, He is Might-y to save, might-y to save, Je - sus is mighty to save. He is might-y to save,

Copyright, 1889, by Wm. J. Kirkpatrick.

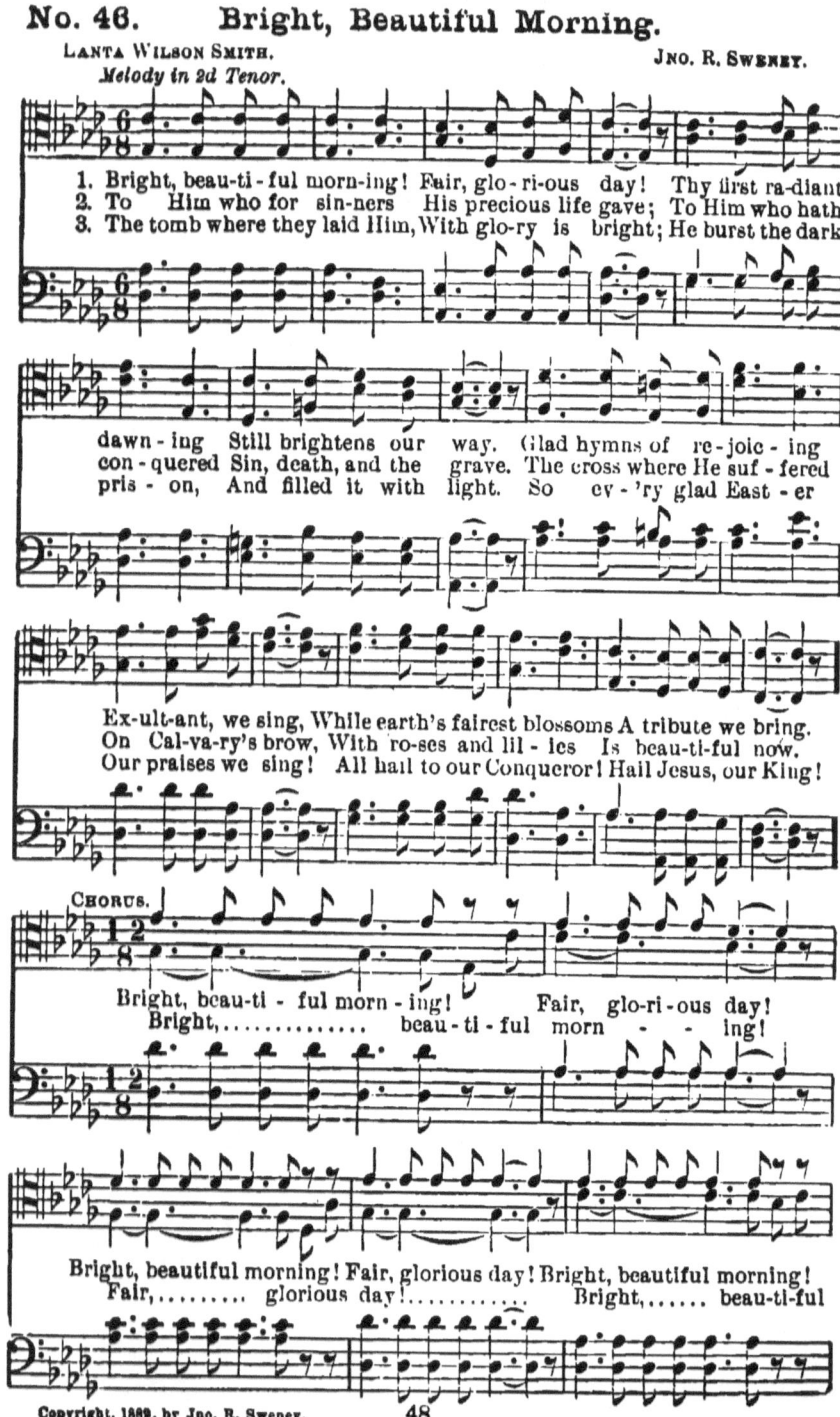

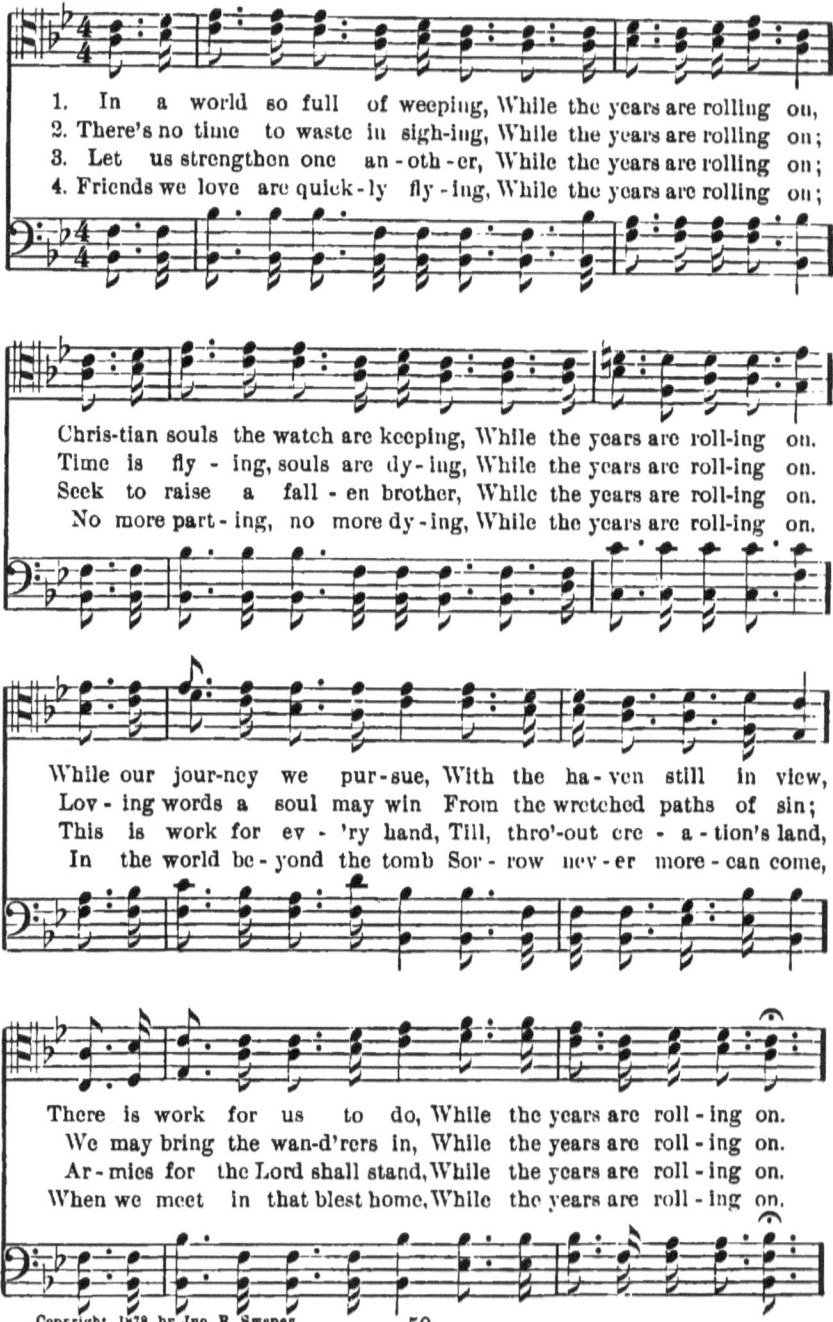

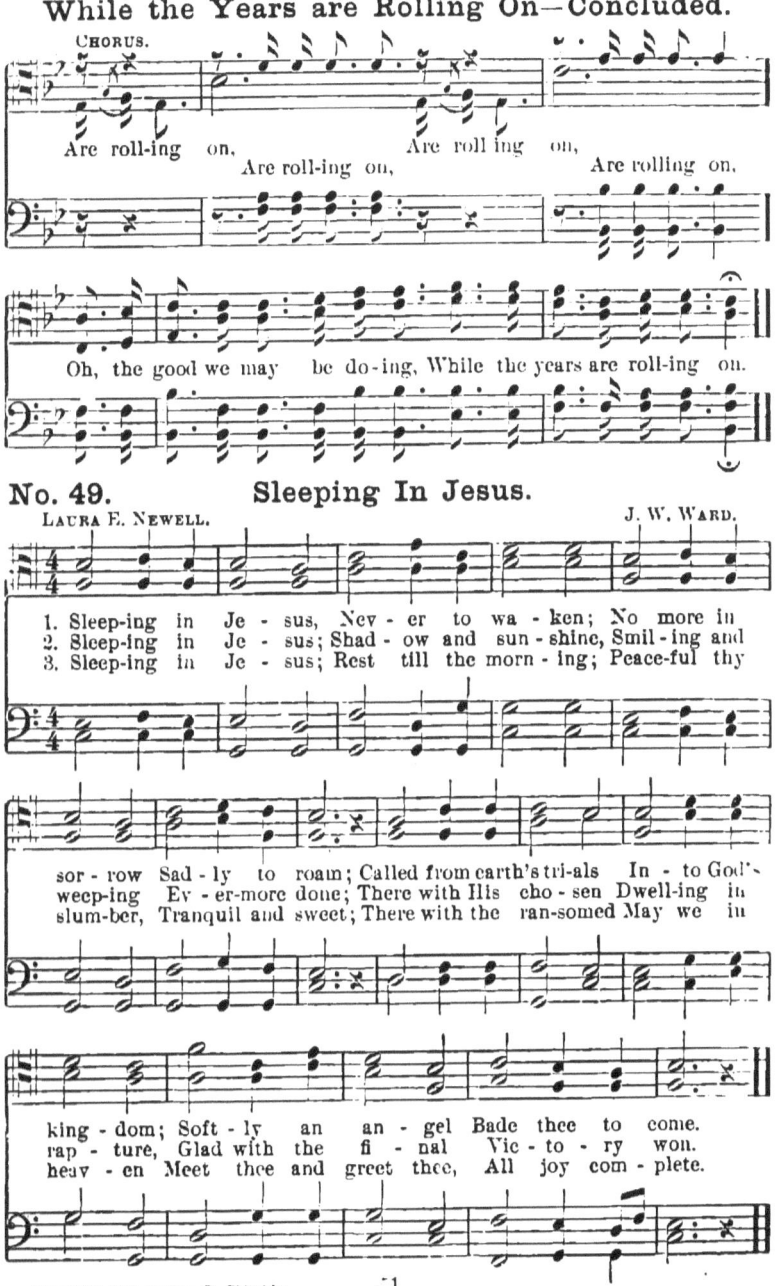

"Eye Hath Not Seen"—Concluded.

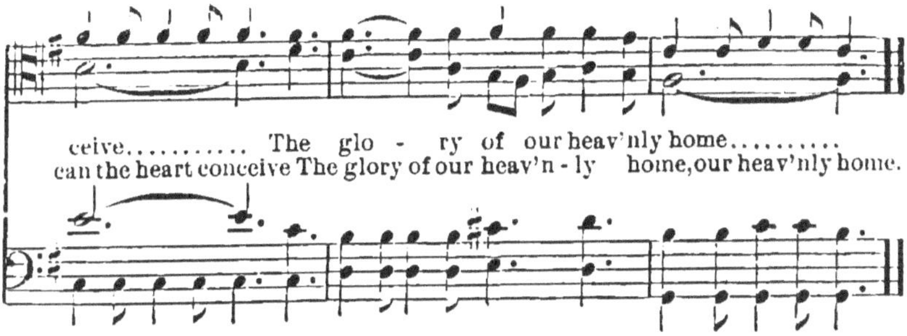

ceive.......... The glo - ry of our heav'nly home..........
can the heart conceive The glory of our heav'n - ly home, our heav'nly home.

No. 51. Come, While the Savior Calls.

FANNY J. CROSBY.   WM. J. KIRKPATRICK.

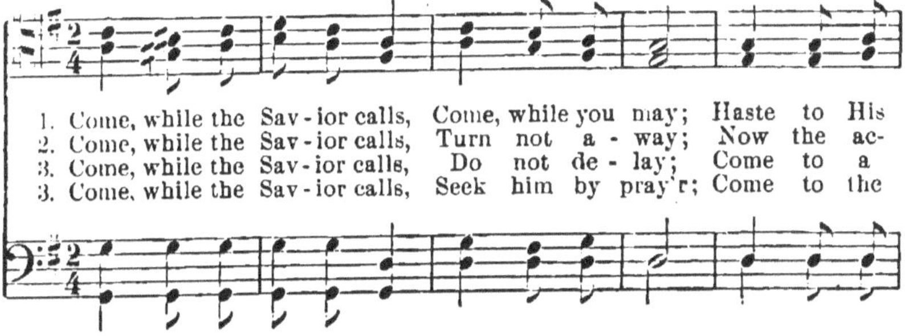

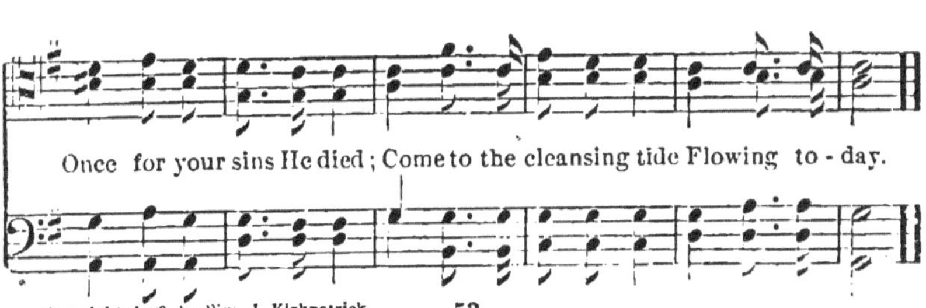

1. Come, while the Sav-ior calls, Come, while you may; Haste to His
2. Come, while the Sav-ior calls, Turn not a - way; Now the ac-
3. Come, while the Sav-ior calls, Do not de - lay; Come to a
3. Come, while the Sav-ior calls, Seek him by pray'r; Come to the

CHORUS.

lov - ing arms; How can you stay?
cept - ed time, Love pleads to - day.
throne of grace, Seek Him to - day.
mer - cy - seat, Je - sus is there.

Once He was cru - ci - fied;
Once for your sins He died; Come to the cleansing tide Flowing to - day.

Copyright, 1888, by Wm. J. Kirkpatrick.

Come, O My Soul—Concluded.

heav'n's tri-um-phant throng Swell at His feet the ev-er-last-ing song.

No. 55. Step Out on the Promise.

E. F. MILLER.

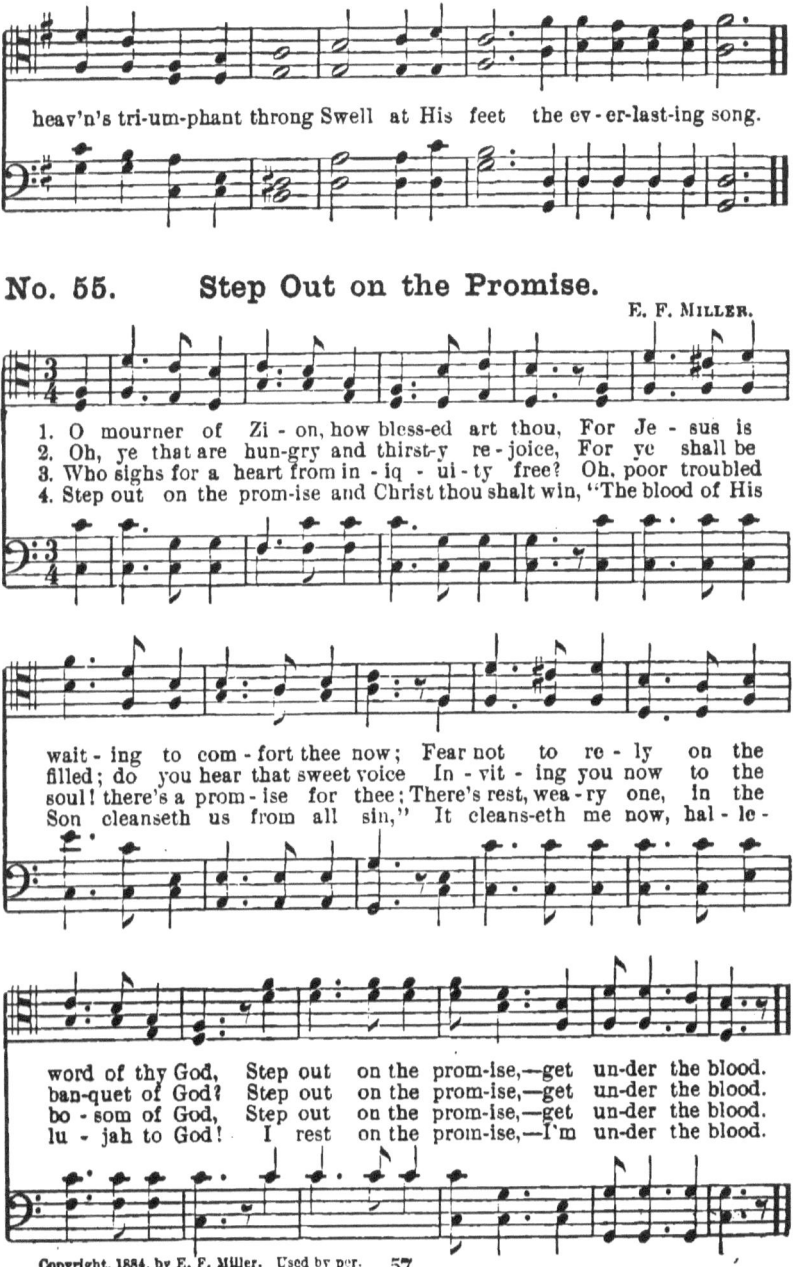

1. O mourner of Zi - on, how bless-ed art thou, For Je - sus is
2. Oh, ye that are hun-gry and thirst-y re - joice, For ye shall be
3. Who sighs for a heart from in - iq - ui - ty free? Oh, poor troubled
4. Step out on the prom-ise and Christ thou shalt win, "The blood of His

wait - ing to com - fort thee now; Fear not to re - ly on the
filled; do you hear that sweet voice In - vit - ing you now to the
soul! there's a prom - ise for thee; There's rest, wea - ry one, in the
Son cleanseth us from all sin," It cleans-eth me now, hal - le -

word of thy God, Step out on the prom-ise,—get un-der the blood.
ban-quet of God? Step out on the prom-ise,—get un-der the blood.
bo - som of God, Step out on the prom-ise,—get un-der the blood.
lu - jah to God! I rest on the prom-ise,—I'm un-der the blood.

Copyright, 1884, by E. F. Miller. Used by per.

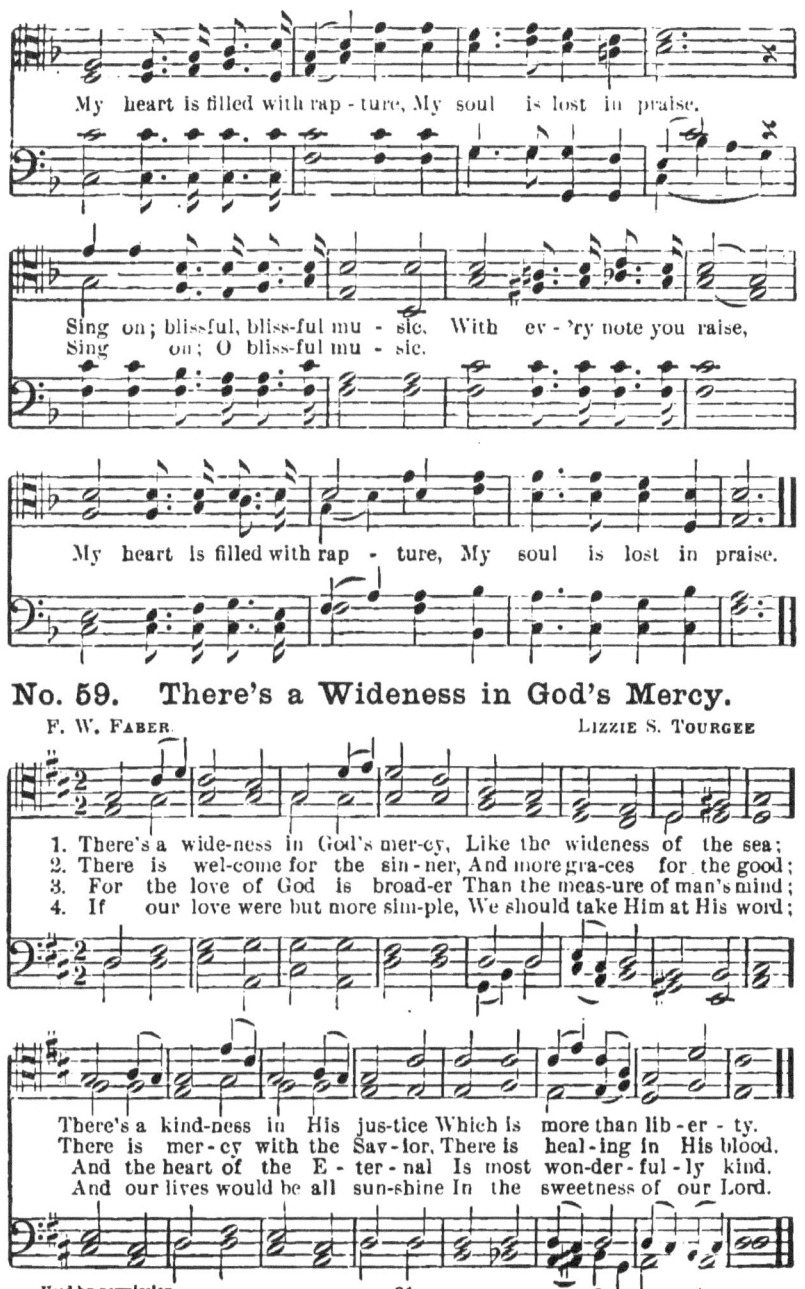

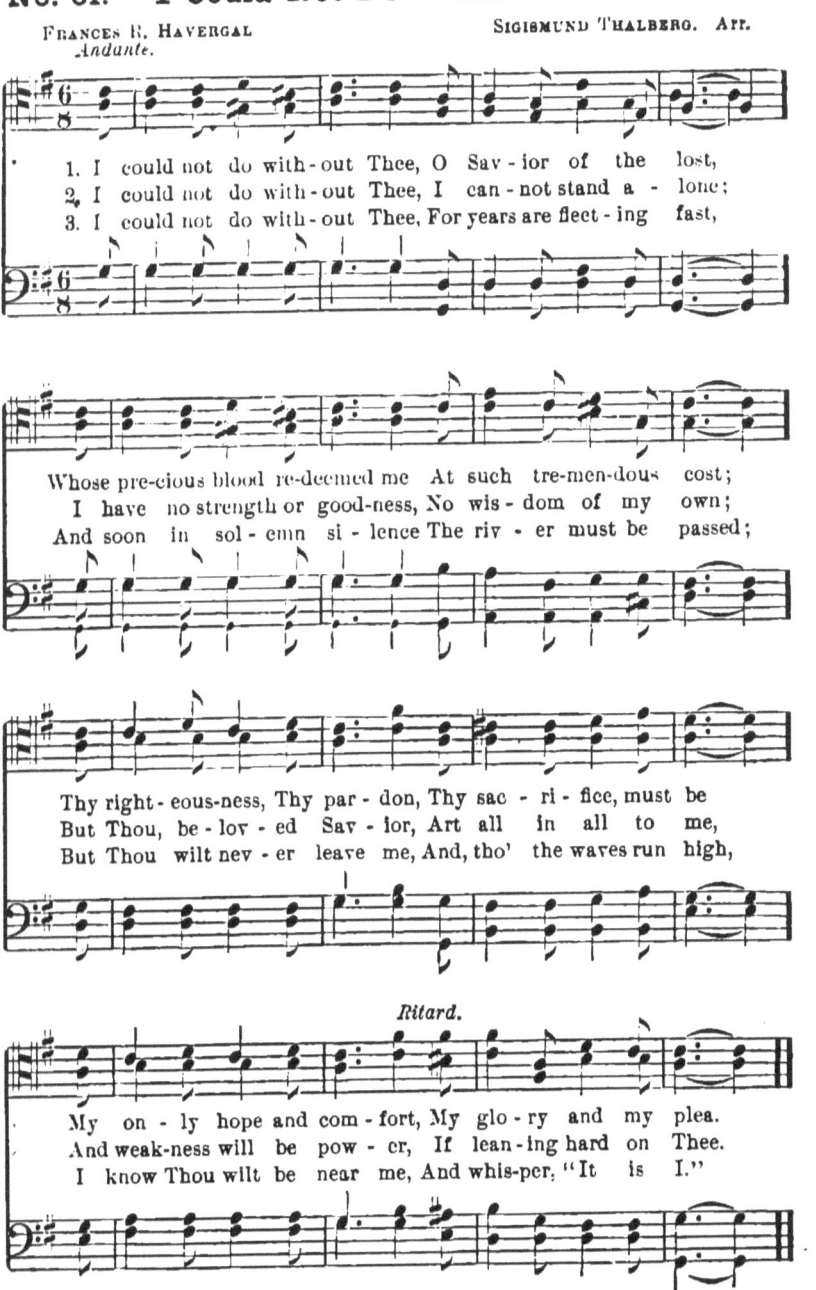

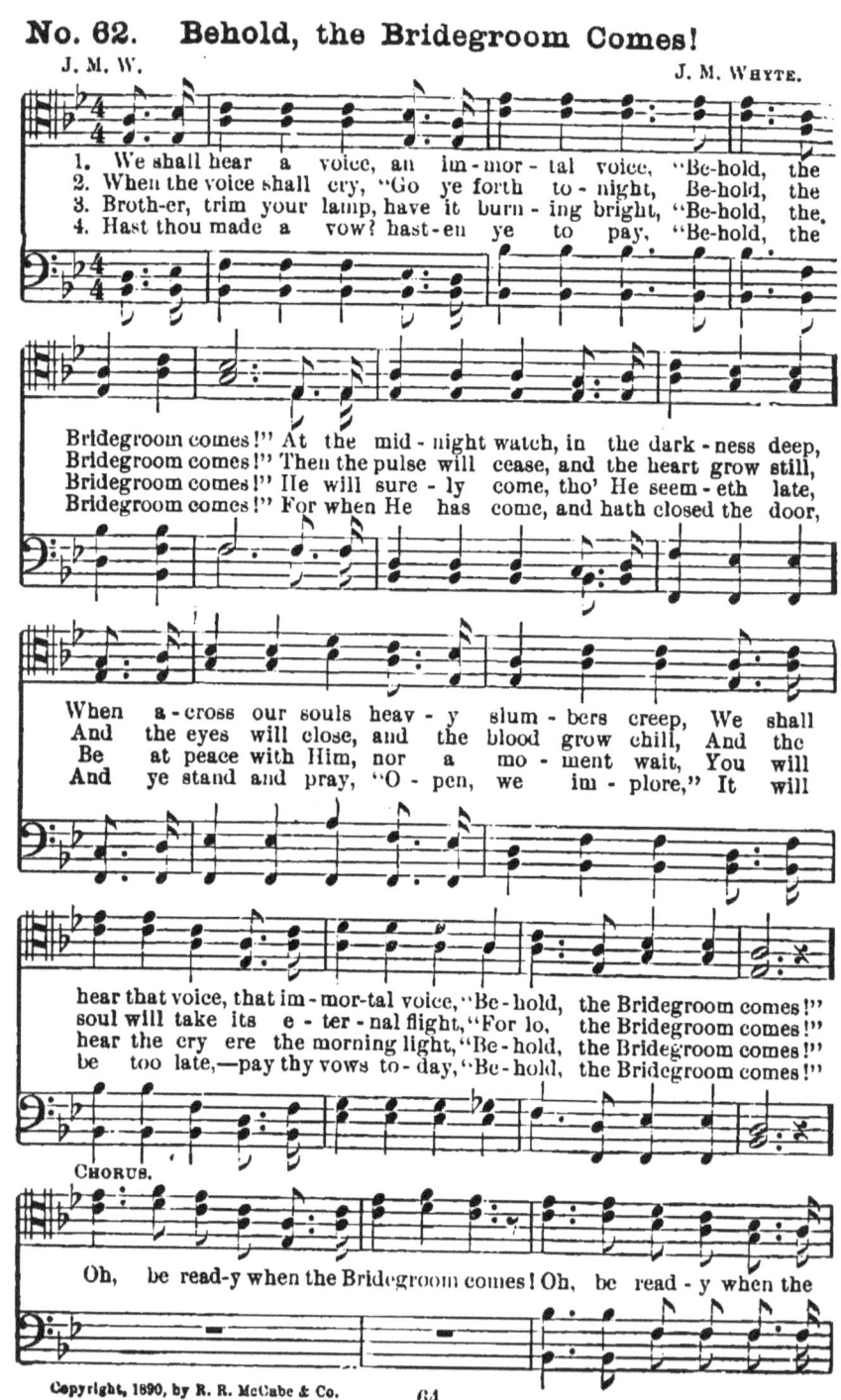

No. 64. Lead Me, Savior.

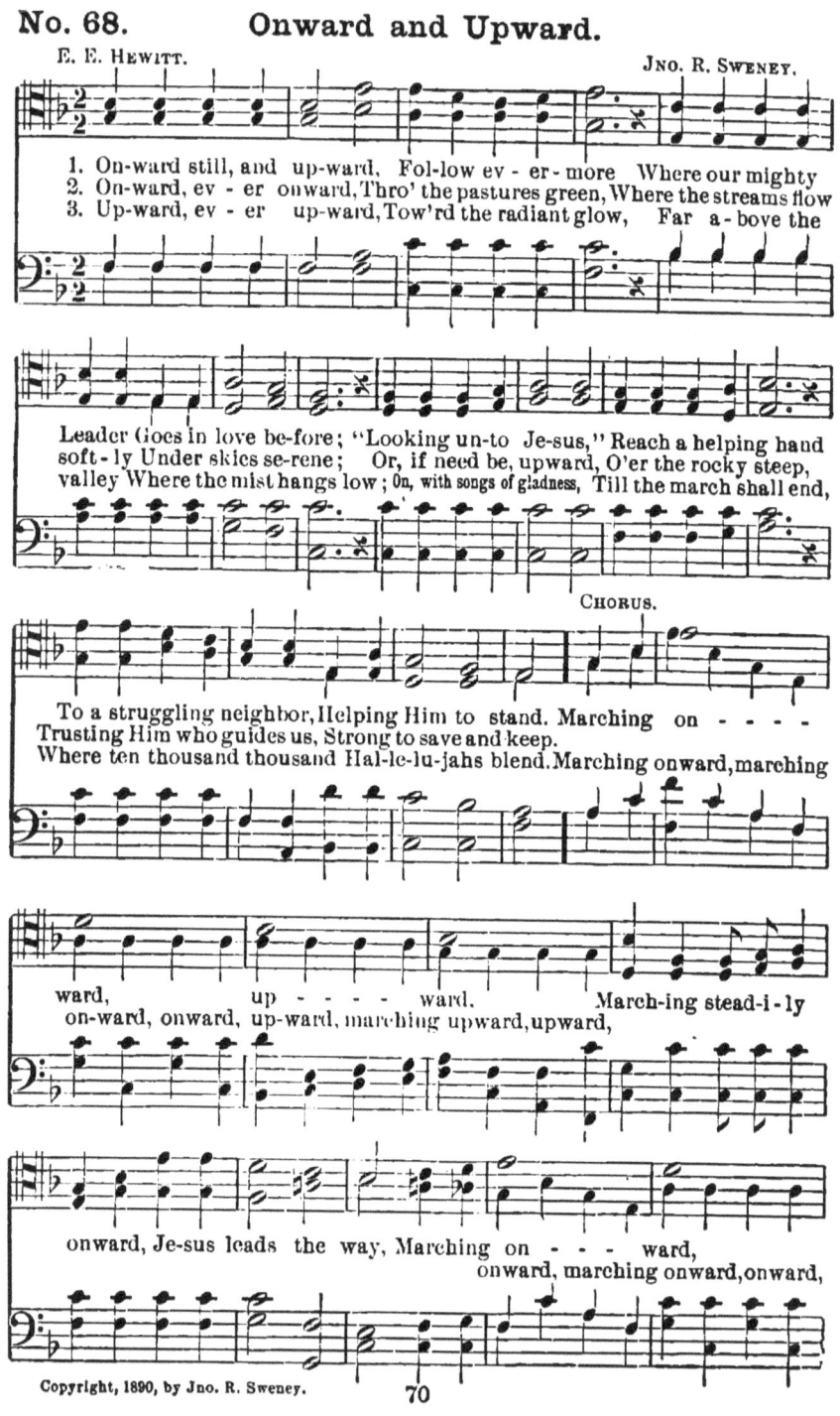

Onward and Upward—Concluded.

up - - - ward, Onward un-to glo-ry, To the per-fect day.
upward, marching upward, upward,

No. 69. The Everlasting Arms.

IDA L. REED.   WM. J. KIRKPATRICK.

1. There's a tho't that cheers me ev - er, Keeps my soul from all a-larms,
2. Tho' the skies are dark a-bove me, Thorn-y be the path be-low,
3. What tho' griefs and care en-cum-ber, Wea-ry bur-dens press me long,
4. Oh, the peace the sweet hope bringeth, And my soul is sat-is-fied,

I shall find e - ter-nal ref - uge In the Ev - er - last-ing Arms.
He will safe - ly keep who loves me, And my soul no fear shall know.
When His kindness I re - mem-ber, This shall ev - er be my song.
And my heart with-in me sing - eth, I shall safe - ly there a - bide.

CHORUS.

In the Ev - er - last-ing Arms, In the Ev - er - last-ing Arms,

We shall find e - ter - nal ref - uge In the Ev-er-last - ing Arms.

Copyright, 1893, by Wm. J. Kirkpatrick.

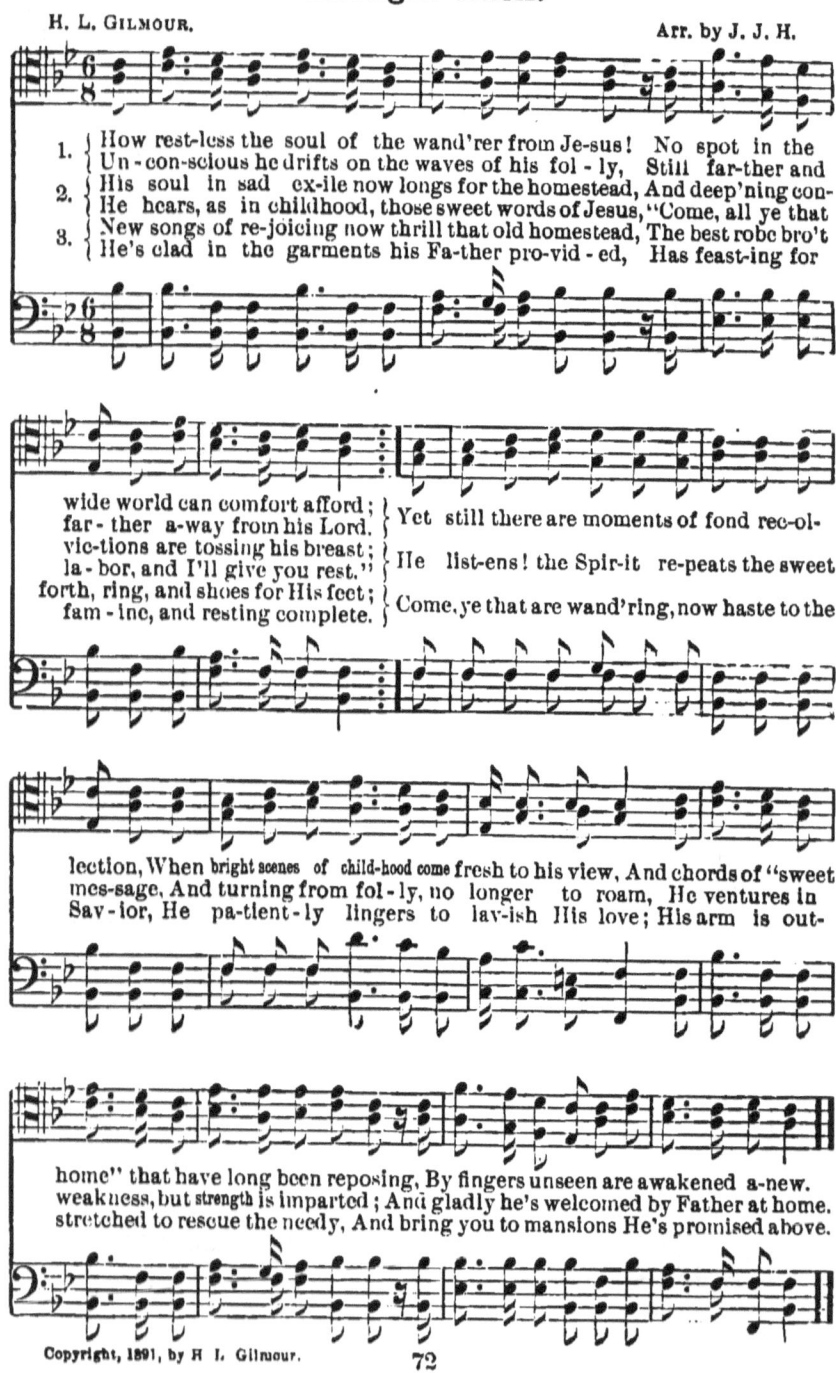

No. 71. **Help Your Brother.**

Mrs. Geo. D. Elderkin.   Jno. R. Sweney.

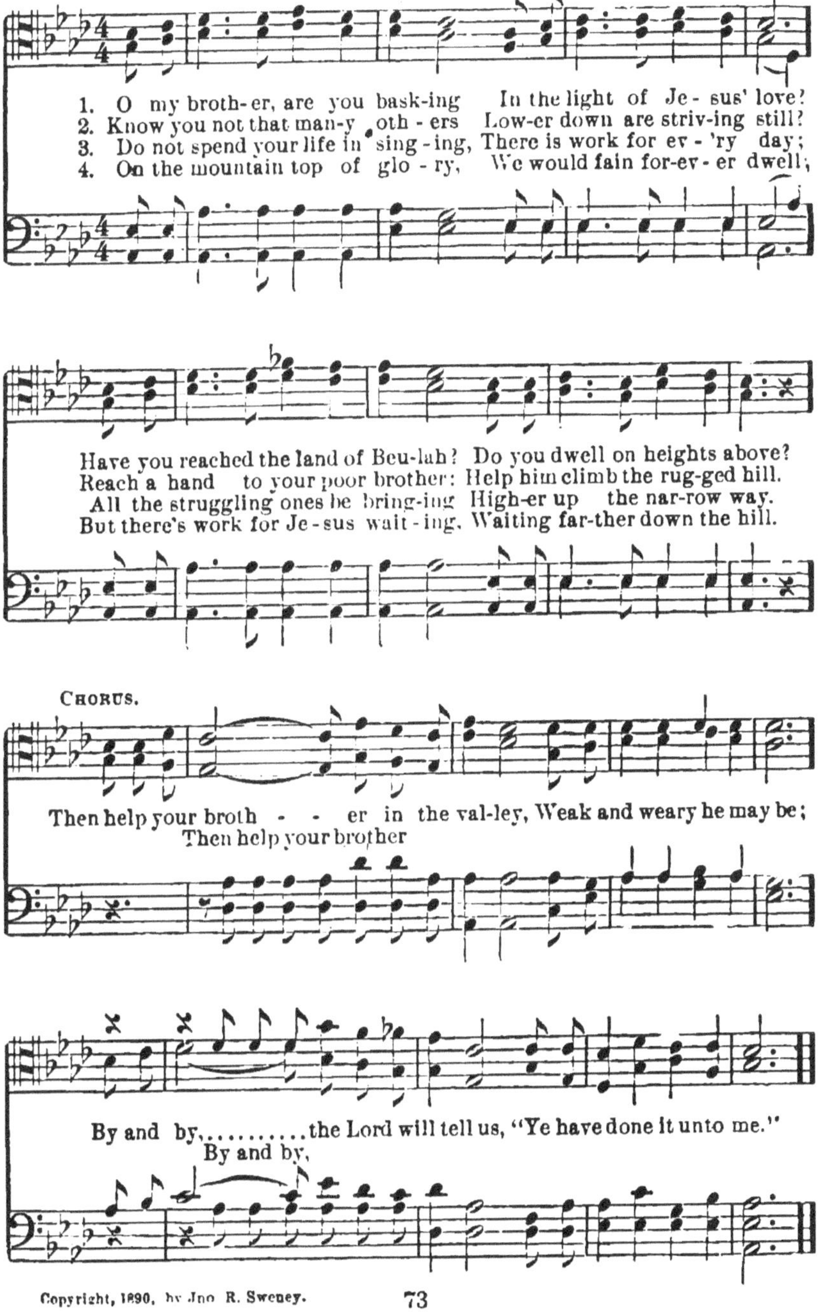

1. O my broth-er, are you bask-ing In the light of Je-sus' love?
2. Know you not that man-y oth-ers Low-er down are striv-ing still?
3. Do not spend your life in sing-ing, There is work for ev-'ry day;
4. On the mountain top of glo-ry, We would fain for-ev-er dwell;

Have you reached the land of Beu-lah? Do you dwell on heights above?
Reach a hand to your poor brother: Help him climb the rug-ged hill.
All the struggling ones be bring-ing High-er up the nar-row way.
But there's work for Je-sus wait-ing. Waiting far-ther down the hill.

CHORUS.

Then help your broth - - er in the val-ley, Weak and weary he may be;
Then help your brother

By and by,..........the Lord will tell us, "Ye have done it unto me."
By and by,

Copyright, 1890, by Jno R. Sweney.

No. 72. One Thing I Know.

E. E. HEWITT.
WM. J. KIRKPATRICK.

Melody in 2d Tenor.

1. One thing I know;....oh, bless His name!... To me the Lord...... of mercy
2. One thing I know;....He heard my cries,... With mighty pow'r He touched my
3. One thing I know;....He died for me,...... In Him my hope,.. my trust shall
4. One thing I know;....the Savior's mine,...Oh, boundless grace,.. oh, joy di-
5. One thing I know;.... oh, help me sing....Such happy praise...to Christ, our

came,...... He filled my heart,...... with love's bright flame,.. This I
eyes,........ To see the light........ that nev-er dies,......... This I
be,........... My Sav-ior lives....... e-ter-nal-ly,......... This I
vine!........ And heav'nly beams..... a-round me shine,...... This I
King........ While smiling faith....... and love up-spring,...... This I

CHORUS.

know,...... this I know. I know, I know.......... He loved me

so,.......... He saved my soul...... from sin and woe,......Now peace and

Copyright, 1893, by Wm. J. Kirkpatrick.

No. 75. Oh, for a Vision of Jesus!

L. H. Edmunds.
Jno. R. Sweney.

1. Oh, for a vi-sion of Je-sus! Oh, for a glimpse of His face,
2. Oh, for a vi-sion of Je-sus! Seen in the won-der-ful Book!
3. Oh, for a vi-sion of Je-sus! When roll the bil-lows of grief!
4. Oh, for a vi-sion of Je-sus! When near the cold Jor-dan-tide!

Cho.—Oh, for a vi-sion of Je-sus! Oh, for a glimpse of His face!

Ra-diant with heav-en-ly glo-ry, Beam-ing with heav-en-ly grace!
As in a clear, shin-ing mir-ror, In those dear pa-ges I look.
O-ver the wa-ters of sor-row, Sav-ior, Thy smile brings re-lief,
Mak-ing a path-way of glo-ry, E'en to the bright "other side."

Ra-diant with heav-en-ly glo-ry, Beam-ing with heav-en-ly grace!

Not here to mor-tals 'tis giv-en, Veil-less His beau-ty to see,
There, Lamb of God, is Thy like-ness, There glows Thy im-age di-vine;
One look—the tempest is pass-ing; One word—the waves are at rest;
There in in-ef-fa-ble splen-dor, Man-i-fest, Lord, to our gaze,

D. C. Chorus.

Yet in the soul's con-tem-pla-tion, Show Thy-self, Sav-ior, to me.
So let me gaze till Thy Spir-it, Lord, is re-flect-ed in mine.
Sweet peace beyond un-der-stand-ing, Je-sus is there "man-i-fest."
More than the an-gels, we'll love Thee, More than the ser-a-phim, praise.

Copyright, 1893, by Jno. R. Sweney.

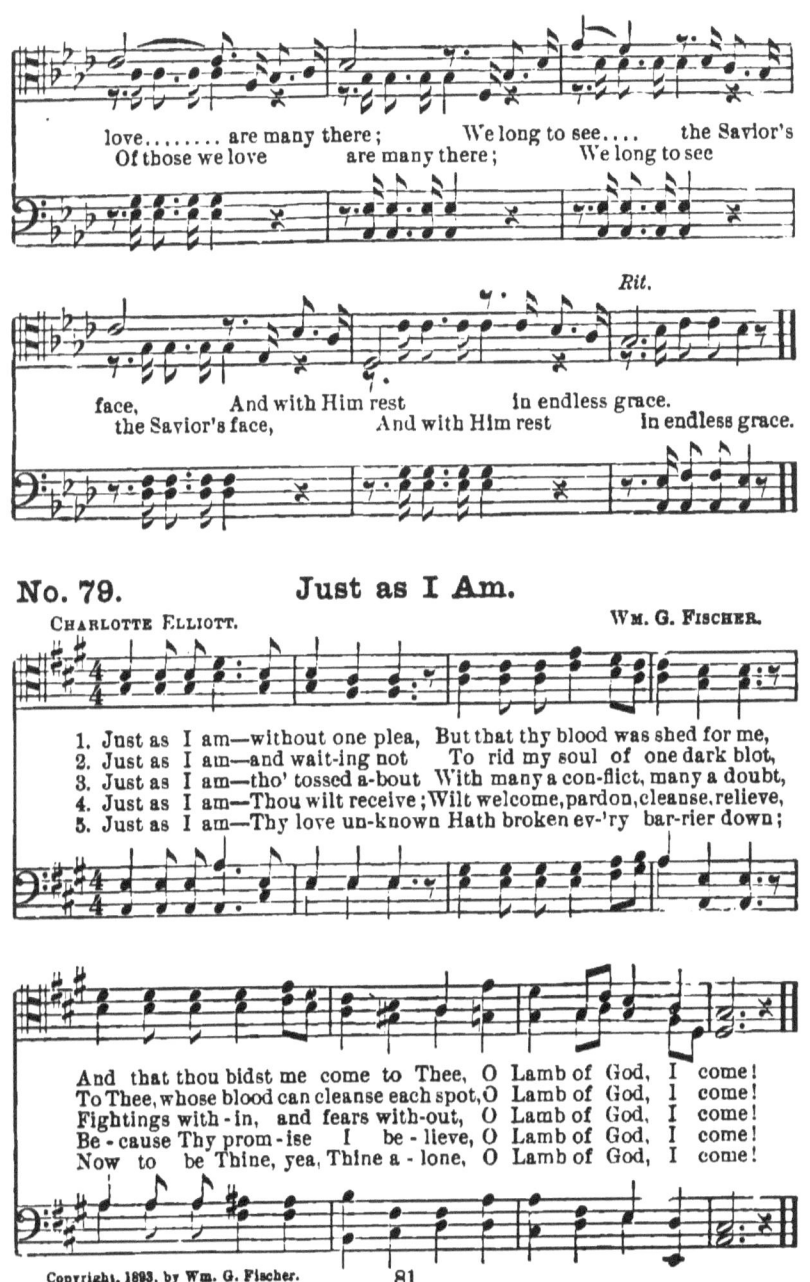

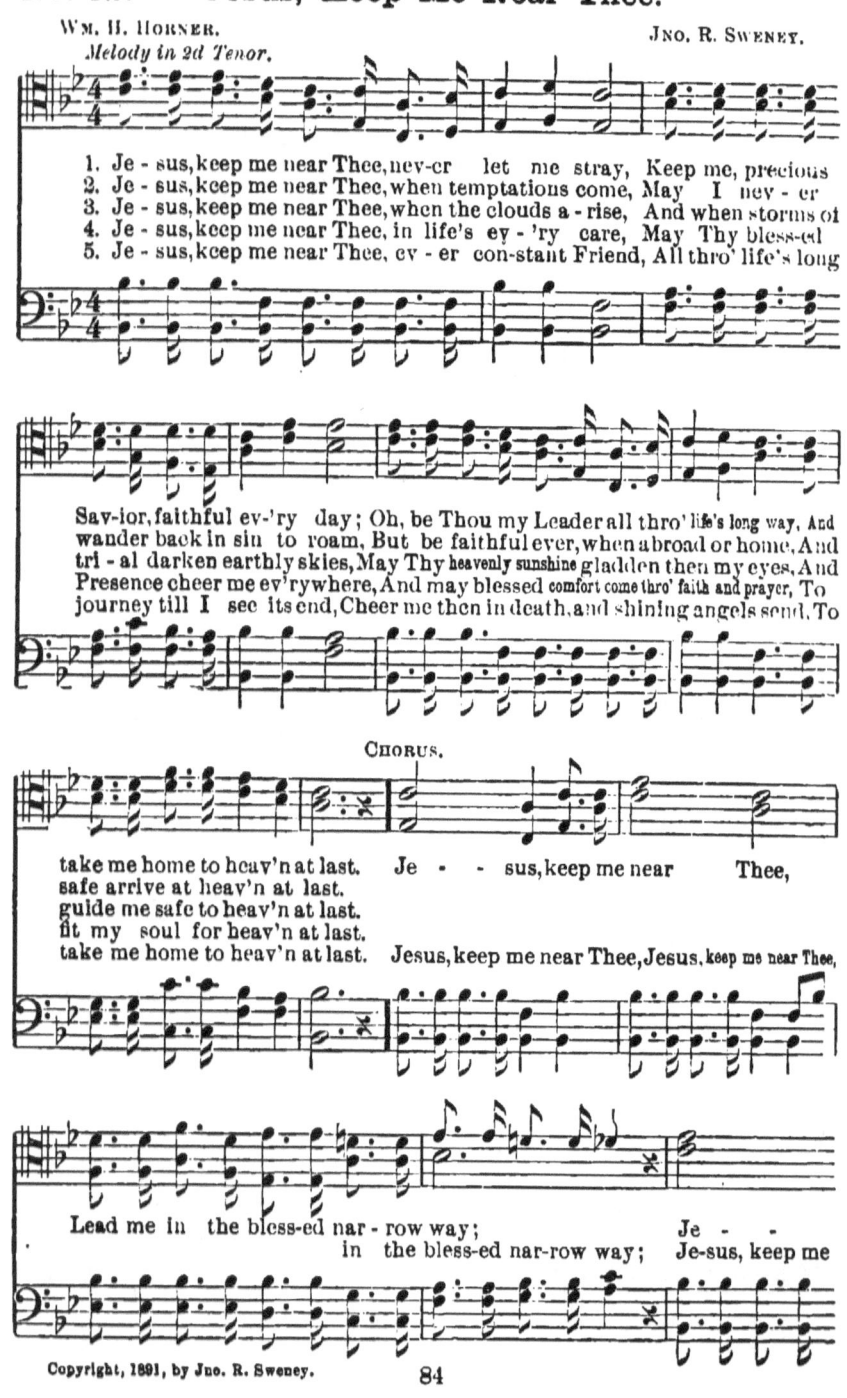

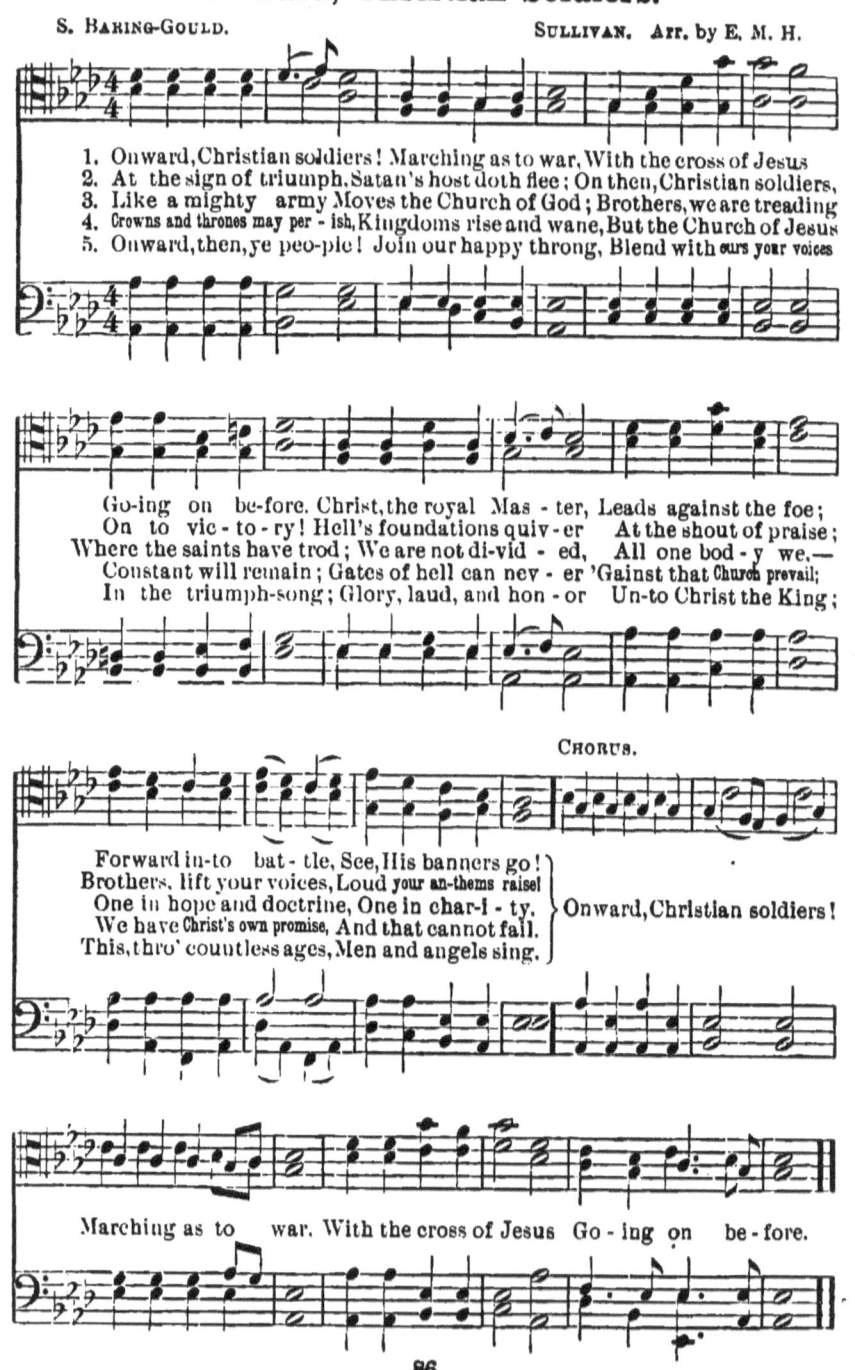

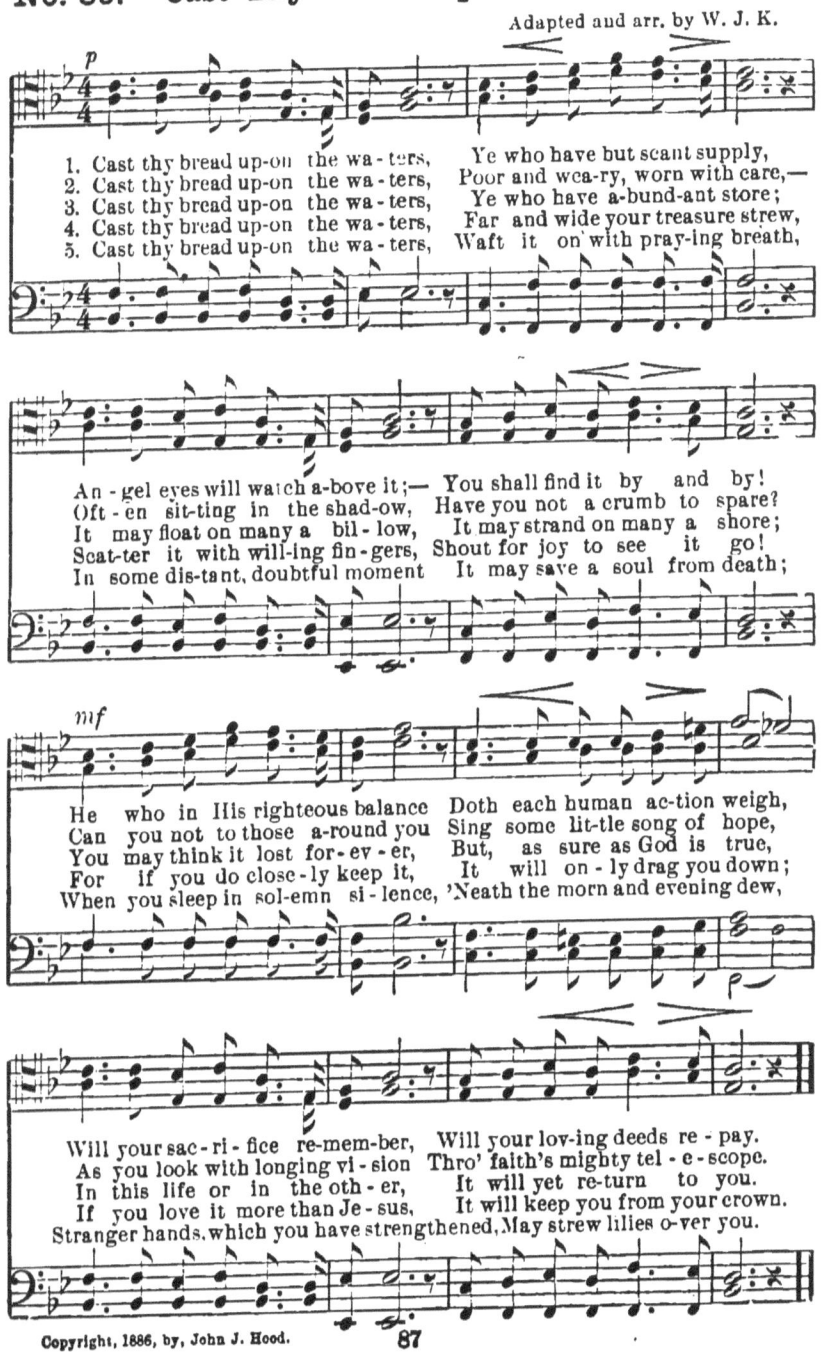

No. 86. Thy Dearest Friend.

Fanny J. Crosby.
Jno. R. Sweney.

1. O troubled heart, behold and see, What grace divine hast done for thee; How, step by step, it leads thy way, To endless joy and perfect day.
2. By cooling streams that murmur low, In dewy meads where flow'rets grow, Beneath His kind and gentle care.
3. Tho' trials oft thy cup may fill, His watchful eye is o'er thee still; He bids thee rest in safety, He will not leave thee here alone.
4. There is a smile for ev'ry tear, A blessed hope for ev'ry fear; Tho' clouds may veil a stormy night, Yet joy will greet the morning light.

CHORUS.
Look up and praise in new-made songs, Thy God to...

Copyright, 1894, by Jno. R. Sweney.

Let Us Hear You Tell It—Concluded.

No. 92. Moments of Blessing.

FANNY J. CROSBY.   JNO. R. SWENEY.

1. Rich are the moments of blessing Jesus, my Savior, bestows;
2. Rich are the moments of blessing, Lovely, and hallowed, and sweet.
3. Why should I ev-er grow weary? Why should I faint by the way?
4. Tho' by the mist and the shadow Sometimes my sky may be dim,

Pure is the well of sal-va-tion Fresh from His mer-cy that flows.
When from my la-bor at noon-tide Calm-ly I rest at His feet.
Has He not promised to give me Strength for the toils of the day?
Rich are the moments of blessing Spent in com-mun-ion with Him.

D.S.—*Spreading a beau-ti-ful rain-bow O-ver the val-ley of tears.*

CHORUS.   D. S.

Ev - er He walketh beside me, Bright-ly His sunshine appears,
Ever, yes, ever He walketh beside me, Brightly His sunshine, His sunshine ap-pears,

Copyright, 1888, by Jno. R. Sweney.

No. 93. Calvary, Dear Calvary!
(Tune on opposite page.)

1 When I survey the wondrous cross
  On which the Prince of Glory died,
My richest gain I count but loss,
  And pour contempt on all my pride.
CHO.-O Calvary! dear Calvary!
  My longing heart is turned to Thee;
O Calvary! dear Calvary!
  Speak to my heart from Calvary.

2 On Calvary's brow my Savior died;
  'Twas there my Lord was crucified;

'Twas on the cross He bled for me,
  And purchased there my pardon free.

3 See, from His head, His hands, His feet,
  Sorrow and love flow mingled down;
Did e'er such love and sorrow meet,
  Or thorns compose so rich a crown.

4 O Jesus, Lord, how can it be [me;
  That Thou shouldst give Thy life for
To bear the cross and agony,
  In that dread hour on Calvary!

No. 94. The Winds were Hushed.

E. E. Hewitt.   Wm. J. Kirkpatrick.

1. Oh, the winds were hushed, and the night grew fair, When the Master's voice brought a bless-ing there: The dark-roll-ing sea owned His sov'reign will, For the might-y King uttered, "peace, be still," For the might-y King ut-tered, "peace, be still."
2. So the heart is hushed in the storm of grief, When the Master's word brings its sweet re-lief; Oh, trust, wea-ry soul, in His ho-ly will, For the King of Love whispers, "peace, be still," For the King of Love whispers, "peace, be still."
3. There's a song of joy when that voice is heard, And new faith upsprings at His bless-ed word; Sing on, hap-py heart, and His praise ful-fill, For the King of Love whispers, "peace, be still," For the King of Love whispers, "peace, be still."

CHORUS.

Peace-ful-ly, peace-ful-ly, peacefully rest, "Child of the King," on His gen-tle breast; Peace-ful-ly, peace-ful-ly,

Copyright, 1893, by Wm. J. Kirkpatrick.

That Beautiful Land—Concluded.

paved with pure gold, And the sun it shall nev-er go down.

No. 99. What Will it Matter.

FANNY J. CROSBY.
Melody in 2d Tenor.
WM. J. KIRKPATRICK.

1. What will it matter, by and by, What will it matter, by and by, Whether my
2. What will it matter, by and by, What will it matter, by and by, Whether my
3. What will it matter, by and by, What will it matter, by and by, Whether the
4. What will it matter, by and by, What will it matter, by and by, Whether

crosses were heav-y or light, Whether my pathway was cloudy or bright,
tri-als were ma-ny or few, Whether the world was unfaithful or true,
wa-ters were bit-ter or sweet, Murmuring gently or sad at my feet,
pass with the morning away. Whether at noontide or clos-ing of day.

Cres.   *pp*   *Ad lib.*

When I shall walk with the ransomed in white, Safe in that beautiful land?
When my Redeemer in glo-ry I view, Home in that beautiful land?
When the departed, with rapture, I meet, Home in that beautiful land?
When in the val-ley of E-den I stray, Home in that beautiful land?

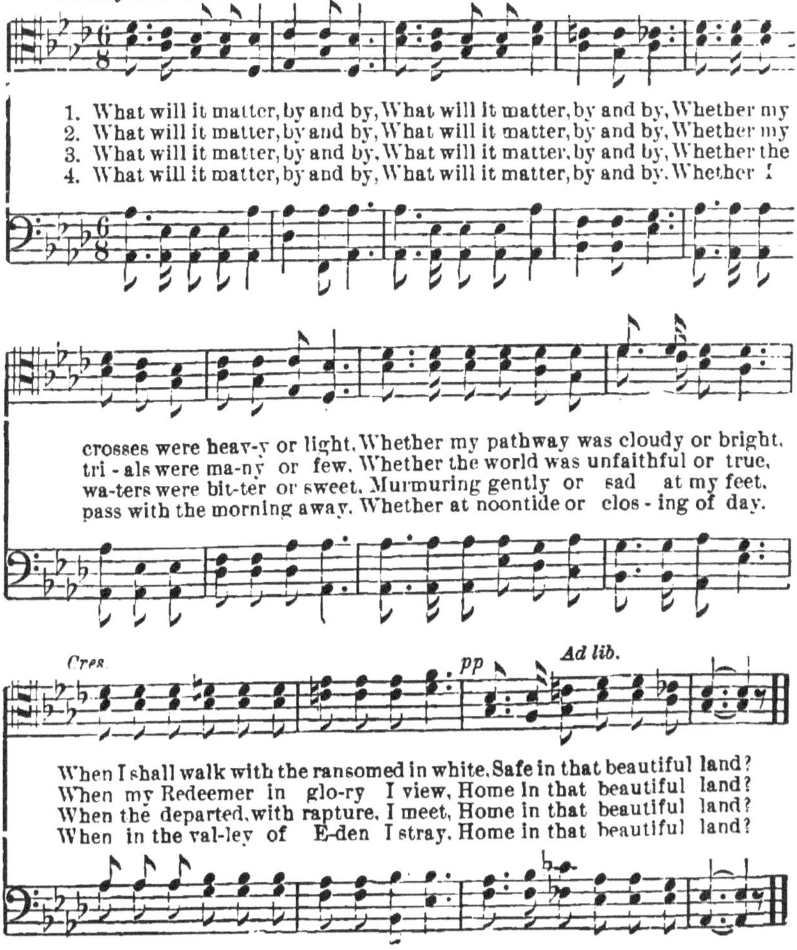

Copyright, 1894, by Wm. J. Kirkpatrick.

INDEX.

Titles in SMALL CAPITALS; First lines in Roman.

	No.		No.
ANGELS ABOVE ARE SINGING	42	I COULD NOT DO WITHOUT THEE	61
A SONG IN MY HEART	26	IF ANY MAN THIRST	39
A wonderful Savior is Jesus	81	I have heard of a land	98
		I HEARD THE VOICE OF JESUS SAY	34
BEAUTIFUL LAND	20	I KNOW THAT MY REDEEMER LIVES	33
BEAUTIFUL ROBES	40	IMMANUEL'S LAND	76
BEHOLD, THE BRIDEGROOM COMES	62	I must have the Savior with me	11
BLESS THE LORD, MY SOUL	28	In a world so full of weeping	48
BRIGHT, BEAUTIFUL MORNING	46	IN THAT CITY	1
BROKEN HEARTS	10	IN THE MORNING	80
BROUGHT BACK	70	In Thy perfect peace divine	25
		IN THE SHADOW OF THY WING	65
CALVARY, DEAR CALVARY	93	In the silent hours of darkness	56
CAST THY BREAD UPON THE WATERS	85	I sang one day a sad sweet song	36
CAST THY BURDEN ON THE LORD	95	I SHALL BE SATISFIED	100
CLOSE THY HEART NO MORE	17	IT WAS SPOKEN FOR THE MASTER	24
COME, O MY SOUL	54	I've wandered far away from God	31
COME TO THE FEAST	67	JESUS FOR ME	2
COME, WHILE THE SAVIOR CALLS	51	JESUS, I COME TO THEE	87
COMING TO-DAY	23	Jesus is the light, the way	12
Conquering now and still to conquer	32	Jesus is waiting His grace to bestow	44
		JESUS, KEEP ME NEAR THEE	82
Day is dying in the west	35	JESUS LEADS	9
DRIFTING	83	Jesus, my Savior, is all things	2
		JESUS SAVES	60
Each cooing dove and sighing	91	JESUS, SAVIOR, PILOT ME	21
EYE HATH NOT SEEN	50	JUST AS I AM	79
FOR YOU AND FOR ME	14	KEEP ME EVER	25
FROM THE STRANGER-COUNTRY	4		
		LEAD, KINDLY LIGHT	89
GOD BLESS MY BOY	30	LEAD ME, SAVIOR	64
		LET US HEAR YOU TELL IT	90
Hark! from the joy-land	8	Life wears a different face to me	57
HARK! HARK, MY SOUL	38	LIGHT AFTER DARKNESS	29
Hark the song of holy rapture	77	Like a shepherd, tender, true	9
HE HIDETH MY SOUL	81	Like the music of a fountain	10
HELP YOUR BROTHER	71	LORD, I'M COMING HOME	31
HE'S MIGHTY TO SAVE	44	LO, THE GOLDEN FIELDS ARE SMILING	97
He that dwelleth in the presence	65		
HIS CHILD FOREVERMORE	88		
Ho! every one that thirsteth	67	MEMORIES OF GALILEE	91
HOME AT LAST	77	MOMENTS OF BLESSING	92
HOME OF THE SOUL	78	MY JESUS, I LOVE THEE	74
How restless the soul of the wanderer	70	MY MOTHER'S BIBLE	16
		MY SOUL SHOUTS GLORY	6

INDEX.

Title	No.
No, Not Despairingly	19
No Shelter but in Christ	15
Not a sound invades the stillness	13
Now the Day is Over	63
O brother, have you told	90
O'er death's sea, in yon blest city	1
Of Him I boast, who shed for me	88
Oft have I heard a voice that said	37
Oh, for a Vision of Jesus	75
Oh, homeland of the true and faithful	78
Oh, my friend, so far from mother	96
Oh, the day of joy that's coming	73
Oh, the winds were hushed	94
O my brother, are you basking	71
O mourner of Zion, how blessed art thou	55
One Thing I Know	72
On the mount of wondrous glory	45
Onward and Upward	68
Onward, Christian Soldiers	84
Onward still, and upward	68
O troubled heart, behold and see	86
Our friends on earth we meet with	47
Out on the desert, looking, looking	23
Praise Him for His glory	28
Prayer is the key	41
Remembered Blessings	36
Rest, Sweet Rest	8
Rich are the moments of blessing	92
Savior, lead me, lest I stray	64
Send Afar the Gospel Tidings	5
Send Out the Sunlight	43
Since I Found my Savior	57
Sing On	58
Sing on, ye joyful pilgrims	58
Sleeping in Jesus	49
Softly and tenderly Jesus is calling	14
Some Blessed Day	27
Some day, but when I cannot tell	27
Speed Away! Speed Away	7
Step Out on the Promise	55
That Beautiful Land	98
The Beautiful Light	12
The City Beyond	18
The Coming Day	73
The Everlasting Arms	69
The Golden Key	41
The Lord Bless Thee	101
The Lord is My Shepherd	3
There is no shelter for the soul	15
There's a dear and precious book	16
There's a song in my heart	26
There's a tho't that cheers me ever	69
There's a Wideness in God's Mercy	59
The sands of time are sinking	76
The Savior With Me	11
The Two Paths	66
The Waiting Savior	56
The Winds were Hushed	94
Though my sins were once like crimson red	53
Tho' Your Sins be as Scarlet	22
Thy Dearest Friend	86
Twilight	35
Two paths lie before you	66
Valley of Eden, beyond the sea	52
Valley of Rest	52
Victory through Grace	32
Washed White as Snow	53
We are pilgrims looking home	80
Weary child, thy sin forsaking	17
Weary pilgrim on life's pathway	95
We have heard the joyful sound	60
We'll Never Say Good-by	47
We'll sing of the statutes divine	18
We shall hear a voice	62
We shall walk with Him in white	40
What Will it Matter	99
When I shall wake in that fair morn	100
When I survey the wondrous cross	93
When shining stars their vigils keep	30
Wherefore art thou wrapt in slumber	88
Where is my Soul To-night	37
While the Years are Rolling On	48
Whisperings of Jesus	13
Wondrous Glory	45
Write a Letter to Your Mother	96

www.ingramcontent.com/pod-product-compliance
Lightning Source LLC
Chambersburg PA
CBHW020154170426
43199CB00010B/1026